Also by Mark Myers

A Smarter Way to Learn JavaScript

The new tech-assisted approach that requires half the effort

1 Read a 10-minute chapter of this book to get each concept.

2 Make the knowledge stick. Do the chapter's free interactive exercises at ASmarterWayToLearn.com.

Mark Myers

Also by Mark Myers

A Smarter Way to Learn jQuery

Learn it faster. Remember it longer.

Mark Myers

1.1

http://www.ASmarterWayToLearn.com

Contents

LEARN IT FASTER.
REMEMBER IT LONGER.

If you embrace this method of learning, you'll get the hang of jQuery in less time than you might expect. And the knowledge will stick.

You'll catch onto concepts quickly.

You'll be less bored, and might even be excited. You'll certainly be motivated.

You'll feel confident instead of frustrated.

You'll remember the lessons long after you close the book.

Is all this too much for a book to promise? Yes, it is. Yet I can make these promises and keep them, because this isn't just a book. It's a book plus 1,500 interactive online exercises. I've done my best to write each chapter so it's easy for anyone to understand, but it's the exercises that are going to turn you into a real jQuery coder.

Cognitive research shows that reading alone doesn't buy you much long-term retention. Even if you read a book a second or even a third time, things won't improve much, according to research.

And forget highlighting or underlining. Marking up a book gives us the illusion that we're engaging with the material, but studies show that it's an exercise in self-deception. It doesn't matter how much yellow you paint on the pages, or how many times you review the highlighted material. By the time you get to Chapter 50, you'll have forgotten most of what you highlighted in Chapter 1.

This all changes if you read less and do more—if you read a short passage and then immediately put it into practice. Washington University researchers say that being asked to retrieve information increases long-term retention by four hundred percent. That may seem implausible, but by the time you finish this book, I think you'll believe it.

Practice also makes learning more interesting.

Trying to absorb long passages of technical material puts you to sleep and kills your motivation. Ten minutes of reading followed by twenty minutes of challenging practice keeps you awake and spurs you on.

And it keeps you honest.

If you *only* read, it's easy to kid yourself that you're learning more than you are. But when you're challenged to produce the goods, there's a moment of truth. You *know* that you know—or that you don't. When you find out that you're a little shaky on this point or that, you can review the material, then re-do the exercise. That's all it takes to master this book from beginning to end.

I've talked with many readers who say they thought they had a problem understanding technical concepts. But what looked like a comprehension problem was really a retention problem. If you get to Chapter 50 and everything you studied in Chapter 1 has faded from memory, how can you understand Chapter 50, which depends on your knowing Chapter 1 cold? The read-then-practice approach embeds the concepts of each chapter in your long-term memory, so you're prepared to tackle material in later chapters that builds on top of those concepts. When you're able to remember what you read, you'll find that you learn jQuery quite readily.

I hope you enjoy this learning approach. And then I hope you go on to set the Internet on fire with some terrific webpages.

HOW TO USE THIS BOOK

Since you may not have learned this way before, a brief user manual might be helpful.

- **Study, practice, then rest.** If you're intent on mastering the fundamentals of jQuery, as opposed to just getting a feel for it, work with this book and the online exercises in a 15-to-30-minute session, then take a break. Study a chapter for 5 to 10 minutes. Immediately go to the online links given at the end of each chapter and code for 10 to 20 minutes, practicing the lesson until you've coded everything correctly. Then take a walk.

- **Don't wear yourself out.** You learn best when you're fresh. If you try to cover too much in one day, your learning will go downhill. Most people find they can comfortably cover one to three chapters a day. Your experience may vary.

- **If you find some of the repetition tiresome, skip exercises.** I wrote the exercises for people like me, who need a lot of repetition. If you're a fast learner or a learner with some coding experience, there's no reason to burden yourself. Click the **Skip Exercise and Get Credit** button to jump ahead. Skip whole sets of exercises if you don't need them. Practice as much as you need to, but no more.

- **If you struggle with some exercises, you know you're *really* learning.** An interesting feature of your brain is that the harder it is for you to retrieve a piece of information, the better you remember it next time. So it's actually good news if you have to struggle to recall something from the book. Don't be afraid to repeat a set of exercises. And consider repeating exercises after letting a few weeks go by. If you do this, you'll be using *spaced repetition*, a power-learning technique that provides even more long-term retention.

- **Do the coding exercises on a physical keyboard.** A mobile device can be ideal for reading, but it's no way to code. Very, very few Web developers would attempt to do their work on a phone. The same thing goes for *learning* to code. Theoretically, most of the interactive exercises could be done on a mobile device. But the idea seems so perverse that I've disabled online practice on tablets, readers, and phones. (It also simplified my own coding work.)

- **If you have an authority problem, try to get over it.** When you start doing the exercises, you'll find that I can be a pain about insisting that you get every little detail right. For example, if you omit a semicolon, the program monitoring your work will tell you the code isn't correct, even though it might run. Learning to write code with precision helps you learn to pay close attention to details, a fundamental requirement for coding in any language.

- **Subscribe, temporarily, to my formatting biases.** Current code formatting is like seventeenth-century spelling. Everyone does it his own way. There are no universally accepted standards. But in the exercises, the algorithms that check your work need standards. They can't grant you the latitude that a human teacher could, because, let's face it, algorithms aren't that bright. So I've had to settle on certain conventions. All of the conventions I teach are embraced by a large segment of the coding community, so you'll be in good company. But that doesn't mean you'll be married to my formatting biases forever. When you begin coding projects, you'll soon develop your own opinions or join an organization that has a stylebook. Until then, I'll ask you to make your code look like my code.

THE LANGUAGE YOU'RE LEARNING HERE

jQuery is a JavaScript library. That is, it's a collection of JavaScript routines that do all kinds of things for you without requiring you to write the underlying JavaScript code. It's a kind of shorthand. It's a robot that codes JavaScript.

Like JavaScript, jQuery must always be linked to by the HTML file that's creating the webpage. You'll learn how to write this link in Chapter 27.

It's good to have some knowledge of JavaScript when you're learning jQuery, but plenty of people don't. You *will* need to understand the fundamentals of HTML and CSS, though, in order to understand jQuery. If HTML or CSS aren't in your toolkit, it might be a good idea to put this book aside for a few weeks and start with my "A Smarter Way to Learn HTML & CSS."

1
TARGET AND ACTION

Let's say you want to give the user the option to convert your webpage to text-only. The user clicks a button, and all the images on the page vanish.

In a later chapter I'll tell you about the code for the button.

For now, take a look at the jQuery code that hides all the images:

```
$("img").hide();
```

The statement has four parts.

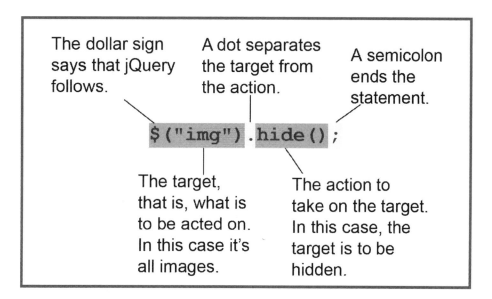

Things to notice:

- The statement begins with a dollar sign. This alerts the program that jQuery follows. It's like saying, "The following statement is in French: *Bonjour, Madame.*" The target—the thing or things to be acted on—begins with the dollar sign. Then there's a pair of parentheses. Within the parentheses is a CSS selector (or possibly more than one) enclosed in quotation marks. In the example, the CSS selector is **img**. No particular image has been selected, so the target comprises all the images on the page.

The jQuery selector comprises the dollar sign, the parentheses, the pair of quotation marks and the CSS selector, **img**.

The jQuery selector tells jQuery which element or elements on the page to select for the action that follows. More examples: **$("p")** selects paragraphs, **$("h2")** selects next-to-largest headings, **$("div")** selects divs, **$("div, p")** selects both divs and paragraphs, **$("ul")** selects unordered lists. In each case, the heart of the jQuery selector is a CSS selector: **p**, **h2**, **div**, **ul**.

- A dot separates the selector from the action.

- The action. Technically, it's known as a *method*. When I write **hide()**, I'm asking jQuery to hide the target. Note that the method ends with a pair of parentheses.

A semicolon marks the end of the *statement*. It's like a period that marks the end of a sentence in a spoken language.

Alternatives to be aware of

Instead of writing...

```
$("img").hide();
```

...you can write...

```
jQuery("img").hide();
```

...or you can write...

```
window.$("img").hide();
```

...or...

```
window.jQuery("img").hide();
```

In this book and the online exercises that accompany it, I'll stick with the dollar sign. I won't test you on the alternatives.

Find the interactive coding exercises for this chapter at:
http://www.ASmarterWayToLearn.com/jquery/1.html

2
ADD CLASSES

You're going to give the user the option of doubling the text size of all the paragraphs on the page so they're easier to read. There will be a button to click that allows the user to choose that option. I'll get to the button in a later chapter.

In your CSS file you've coded a class that calls for double the text size.

```
.big {
  font-size: 2em;
}
```

Now here's the jQuery code that assigns the class to all paragraphs on the page, doubling the text size:

```
$("p").addClass("big");
```

The statement has almost the same pattern as the one you learned in the last chapter:

- It starts with a dollar sign, which means that jQuery follows.

- In this case, the CSS selector is **p**, for paragraphs. It's enclosed in quotation marks, and then in parentheses.

- A dot comes after the selector.

- The method name, in this case **addClass**, comes next.

- The statement ends with a semicolon.

But notice a difference. In the statement you learned in the last chapter, the method name was followed by empty parentheses: **hide()**. In this statement, the parentheses enclose the name of the class to be added. Note that the class name is in quotation marks: **addClass("big")**.

addClass means what it says: "*add* a class"—not "*replace* a class." So if an element has already been assigned one or more classes, the new class will be *in addition to* those classes.

You can add more than one class at a time. The following code adds the three classes "big," "bright," and "heavy" to all h2 headings:

```
$("h2").addClass("big bright heavy");
```

Note that all three class names are enclosed in a single set of parentheses. They're separated only by a space. There are no commas.

You can also remove a class (or classes):

```
$("h2").removeClass("big heavy");
```

The code above removes the classes "big" and "heavy."

Find a demo for this chapter at:
http://jsfiddle.net/ASmarterWayToLearn/u47nj5po/.

Find the interactive coding exercises for this chapter at:
http://www.ASmarterWayToLearn.com/jquery/2.html

3
SELECT BY CLASS

In the first two chapters, you selected all elements of a particular type to be acted on. For example, you wrote $("img") to select all images or $("p") to select all paragraphs. You can also select just *some* or just *one* of a particular type.

For example, the following statement adds the class "big" *only to* paragraphs that already have the class "important."

```
$("p.important").addClass("big");
```

Now all paragraphs of the class "important" also have the class "big." If, for example, the class "big" specifies a font-size of 2em, adding that class via jQuery sizes all paragraphs of the class "important" at 2em.

Once again, the heart of the jQuery selector is a CSS selector: **p.important**.

As you know, CSS can define a class that's tied to a particular element, like this:

```
p.important {
  font-family: Arial, Helvetica, sans-serif;
}
```

Or it can define a class that's independent of any particular element types, like this:

```
.important {
  font-family: Arial, Helvetica, sans-serif;
}
```

In CSS, by defining the class as a class of paragraphs, you're saying that the class can be assigned only to paragraphs, not headings or other text elements.

jQuery works the same way. Let's say you've defined a class independent of any particular elements. Then this code...

```
$(".important").addClass("big");
```

...selects all elements of all types that have been assigned the class "important." This may include paragraphs, headings, divs, lists—any elements that contain text.

But if you write...

```
$("p.important").addClass("big");
```

...the statement selects only *paragraphs* of that class, even though there may be other types of elements, such as headings or divs, that have been assigned the class.

Similarly, if you write...

```
$("ul.important").addClass("big");
```

...only unordered lists of that class will be selected, even though there may be other types of elements that have been assigned the class.

Find a demo for this chapter at:
http://jsfiddle.net/ASmarterWayToLearn/bw9xo3do/.

Find the interactive coding exercises for this chapter at:
http://www.ASmarterWayToLearn.com/jquery/3.html

4
SELECT BY ID,
INSERT TEXT AND HTML

You can target a single element by selecting by id. The following code replaces any text in the paragraph whose id is "greeting" with the text "Hello World!"

```
$("#greeting").text("Hello World!");
```

Things to notice:

- Once again, the heart of the jQuery selector is a CSS selector : **#greeting**.

- Again, a dot separates the selector and the method.

- The method is named **text**. It replaces any text in a paragraph whose id is "#greeting."

- As in all methods, parentheses follow the method.

- Within the parentheses, the text to be inserted is in quotation marks.

Instead of specifying only the id, you can include the element type that has the id....

```
$("p#greeting").text("Hello World!");
```

Since an id can apply to only one element on the page, specifying the element isn't necessary, but I like to do it to make things a little clearer for human readers.

Suppose you want to include HTML tags within the paragraph. If you write the following code, expecting jQuery will display the text in bold...

```
$("#greeting").text("<b>Hello World!</b>");
```

...jQuery will disappoint you by displaying...

Hello World!

When you want jQuery to interpret HTML tags *as* HTML tags, instead of using the **text()** method, you write...

```
$("#greeting").html("<b>Hello World!</b>");
```

Now it displays...

Hello World!

Find a demo for this chapter at:
http://jsfiddle.net/ASmarterWayToLearn/gmj3n633/
Find the interactive coding exercises for this chapter at:
http://www.ASmarterWayToLearn.com/jquery/4.html

5

READ WHAT THE USER HAS ENTERED

Let's say you have an email form for the user to fill out. You want to check the email address she's entered so you can make sure it looks like a valid address. For example, you want to be sure it has an *@* and a dot in it. If it doesn't look right, you can display a message that asks her to correct it.

Suppose you've assigned the address field an id of "e_add." Here's the jQuery code for reading what the user has entered in the field:

```
var addressEntered = $("input#e_add").val();
```

Things to notice:

- **var** is the keyword you use to start any variable declaration. It says: "I declare the following to be a variable."

- **addressEntered** **=** says to store the result of the jQuery action in the JavaScript variable **addressEntered**. For example, if the user has entered "me@gmail.com" in the field whose id is "e_add", **addressEntered** now has the value "me@gmail.com." With this data stored in the variable, you can use JavaScript to test it for validity, as I show how to do in Chapter 85 of my "A Smarter Way to Learn JavaScript." If your JavaScript determines that the address looks wrong, the script can alert the user and ask him to re-enter it.

- By now you know what **$("input#e_add")** means: "Select the element with the id of 'e_add'." In this case, the element with that id is the email address field.

- The dot separates the selector from the method.

- **val()** is the method that gets the value—whatever the user has entered in the field. The value in the field is stored in the variable **addressEntered**.

- The semicolon ends the statement.

Find a demo for this chapter at:
http://jsfiddle.net/ASmarterWayToLearn/mtb0t1x4/
Find the interactive coding exercises for this chapter at:
http://www.ASmarterWayToLearn.com/jquery/5.html

6
FILL IN A FORM FIELD FOR THE USER

I feel it's inconsiderate for a webpage to ask me for information that it should know. For example, when I fill out a form giving my ZIP code as 87571, all the webpage has to do is check a ZIP code chart to see that my state is New Mexico.

Let's do this favor for the user. First you capture the entry in the ZIP code field, as you learned to do in the last chapter:

```
var userZIP = $("input#ZIP").val();
```

You find the state that matches the ZIP code in a JavaScript array. (See Chapter 15 of my "A Smarter Way to Learn JavaScript") You store the state in a variable. Let's call the variable matchedState

Then you insert it into the form's state field. (I'm giving the field an id of "userState." in the example.)

```
$("input#userState").val(matchedState);
```

My state, "NM," appears in the state field.

Instead of inserting a string stored in a variable, you can insert a string itself enclosed in quotation marks:

```
$("input#userState").val("NY");
```

You can read the user's input in one field and insert it in a second field:

```
$("input#userState2").val($("input#userState1").val()
);
```

Find a demo for this chapter at:
http://jsfiddle.net/ASmarterWayToLearn/d16hyhz1/
Find the interactive coding exercises for this chapter at:
http://www.ASmarterWayToLearn.com/jquery/6.html

7
SETTING AND GETTING CONTENT: REVIEW PLUS A NEW ONE

In Chapter 4 you learned how to insert content into an element using `text("[content]")` and `html("[content]")`. For example, this code inserts a paragraph, including HTML tags and the text "Hello world!" into the div with an id of "sayHi":

```
$("div#sayHi").html("<p>Hello world!</p>");
```

In Chapter 5, you learned to read the content that the user has entered in the email address field and store it in a variable:

```
var addressEntered = $("input#eAd").val();
```

As you learned in the last chapter, this process can also be reversed, so you're writing instead of reading.

```
$("input#eAd").val("youraddress@whatever.com");
```

The field is now filled with "youraddress@whatever.com."

Here's a new one:

You can reverse the process you learned in Chapter 4, reading rather than writing content. The following statement reads the text in a paragraph and stores it in the variable **whatsThere**.

```
var whatsThere = $("p#intro").text();
```

The following statement reads the HTML, including any tags and any text, in the div, and stores it in the variable **whatsThere**.

```
var whatsThere = $("div#sayHi").html();
```

Find a demo for this chapter at:
http://jsfiddle.net/ASmarterWayToLearn/jw20nb2x/

Find the interactive coding exercises for this chapter at:
http://www.ASmarterWayToLearn.com/jquery/7.html

8
FADE IN AND OUT

For a little extra flair, you can use jQuery to fade elements in and out. This code fades in all divs with a class of "slowAppearing."

```
$("div.slowAppearing").fadeIn();
```

The only thing new here is the method, **fadeIn()**. Note that there's a capital letter in the method name: **fadeIn()**

You can control the speed of the fade, specifying "fast" or "slow." The following code produces a slow fade.

```
$("div.slowAppearing").fadeIn("slow");
```

Note that the speed is enclosed in quotation marks.

For even more control, specify the speed in milliseconds. The following code makes the fade last 2 seconds.

```
$("div.slowAppearing").fadeIn(2000);
```

Note that the number is *not* enclosed in quotation marks.

You can make an element **fadeOut**. The following

code makes divs of the class "slowDisappearing" disappear over the course of 5 seconds.

```
$("div.slowDisappearing").fadeOut(5000);
```

To fade something in, style images in CSS to initially be invisible:

```
img.softEntrance {
   display: none;
}
```

Then, when it's time to make the images visible, fade them in:

```
$("img.softEntrance").fadeIn("fast");
```

Find a demo for this chapter at:
http://jsfiddle.net/ASmarterWayToLearn/Ljq30mmx/
Find the interactive coding exercises for this chapter at:
http://www.ASmarterWayToLearn.com/jquery/8.html

9
WATCH FOR A CLICK

In Chapter 1, I showed you how to make images disappear when a button is clicked. Now we deal with the click.

Let's say you've written this piece of HTML markup:

```
<button id="b1">Click to make pics disappear</button>
```

The markup above creates a button with the id "b1."

Here's how you tell jQuery to listen for the button to be clicked:

```
$("button#b1").on("click"...[continued in the next chapter]
```

In this chapter I'm showing you just the first part of the statement, the part that listens for the click.

Things to notice:

- As usual, the statement begins with a dollar sign followed by the rest of the selector. In this case, the target is the button with an id of "b1." You could shorten the selector by omitting **button**, since the only item with that particular id is a button: **$("~~button~~#b1")**. I prefer to include **button**, to make things clear for humans.

- Next comes a dot, and then on. The word on means "when the following event occurs...."

- Then there's an opening parenthesis, followed by the name of the event, in quotation marks: **("click"**

This code listens for a double click on a heading:

```
$("h2#guarantee").on("dblclick"...
```

This code listens for the user to click in a form field:

```
$("input#age_field").on("focus"...
```

This code listens for the user to click a form's Submit button:

```
$("form#f3").on("submit"...
```

You can ask jQuery to listen for more than one type of event. When any event included in the list occurs, an action is triggered. The following code listens for either a click or a doubleclick:

```
$("button").on("click dblclick"...
```

Note that **click** and **dblclick** are separated by a space. There is no comma. Both are enclosed in a single set of quotation marks.

Find the interactive coding exercises for this chapter at:
http://www.ASmarterWayToLearn.com/jquery/9.html

10

DO SOMETHING WHEN THERE'S A CLICK

In the last chapter I showed you the beginning of an event statement—the part that listens for a click or another event. Here's the rest of it:

```
$("button#b1").on("click", function() {
  $("img").hide();
});
```

Let's take this a little at a time, starting with this:

```
$("button#b1").on("click", function() {
```

After the event name—in this case **"click"**—there's a comma, followed by a mysterious section of code. If you're an experienced coder, you'll recognize this piece of code as an *anonymous function*. Exactly *why* the action to be taken when an event occurs must be packaged as a function is beyond the scope of a book that focuses on syntax. So let's put on our Buddhist hats and accept that this is just the way it is and cheerfully take on the task of memorizing the pattern.

So after the comma, you put in a space, followed by

`function()` {. That's **function**...empty parentheses...and opening bracket. That's the end of the first line.

You already know how to code the next line. It's the dollar sign, followed by the rest of the selector, the dot, and the method, and closed with a semicolon. What's new here is that it's indented two spaces, to show that it's the inner detail of the function.

The last line may look nonsensical at first, but it's just a piece of housekeeping that closes everything up.

The left-facing bracket on the last line closes the opening bracket of the first line.

```
$("button#b1").on("click", function() {
  $("img").hide();
});
```

The left-facing parenthesis on the last line closes the opening parenthesis after on.

```
$("button#b1").on("click", function() {
  $("img").hide();
});
```

And the semicolon marks the end of the block.

```
$("button#b1").on("click", function() {
  $("img").hide();
});
```

An alternative to be aware of

Instead of writing...

```
$("button#b1").on("click", function() {
```

...you can shorten it by writing...

```
$("button#b1").click (function() {
```

Many experts prefer the long version because it requires less processing. That's the version I'll stick with in this book and the exercises.

Find a demo for this chapter at:
http://jsfiddle.net/ASmarterWayToLearn/5tLp4hmb/

Find the interactive coding exercises for this chapter at:
http://www.ASmarterWayToLearn.com/jquery/10.html

11
SLIDE SOMETHING INTO VIEW

The user clicks a button, and an image gradually appears, expanding from nothing to full size. In CSS, the image is styled so it's initially hidden:

```
img#dramatic {
  display: none;
}
```

An HTML tag puts the invisible phantom on the page, along with a button:

```
<img src="slow_loris_1.jpg" width="100" id="dramatic"
height="117" alt="loris 1">
<button id="make_visible">Show the loris.</button>
```

When the button is clicked, jQuery slides the image into view:

```
$("button#make_visible").on("click", function() {
  $("img#dramatic").slideDown();
});
```

You could add another button to make the image slide

up *out* of view:

```
<button id="goAway">Lose the loris.</button>
```

This is the jQuery code:

```
$("button#goAway").on("click", function() {
  $("img#dramatic").slideUp();
});
```

In Chapter 8 you learned how to control the speed of fades by inserting "fast," "slow," or a number of milliseconds inside the parentheses. You can do the same thing with slides. For example:

```
$("img#dramatic").slideDown(1500);
```

The highlighted number is milliseconds. One thousand milliseconds equal one second. The code above says to take 1.5 seconds to complete the slide.

Find a demo for this chapter at:
http://jsfiddle.net/ASmarterWayToLearn/jy780y7m/
Find the interactive coding exercises for this chapter at:
http://www.ASmarterWayToLearn.com/jquery/11.html

12
SHOW AND TOGGLE

In previous chapters you learned various ways to gradually hide and reveal things on the page.

You can also hide and show things instantly. The following code instantly displays a div (including all its contents) that has been hidden:

```
$("div#onceHidden").show();
```

The following code switches back and forth. It makes instantly visible all ordered lists of a certain class if they're hidden—and hides them if they're visible:

```
$("ol.switched").toggle();
```

In earlier chapters you learned that you could control the speed of fades and slides. You can do the same thing with the **hide()**, **show()**, and **toggle()** methods.

When you leave the parentheses empty as in the examples above, the effect is instant.

The following code hides all images on the page by rapidly sliding them up, so the slide is just barely visible:

```
$("img").hide("fast");
```

The following code shows all h2 headings of the class "optional" by slowly sliding them down:

```
$("h2.optional").show("slow");
```

The following code toggles the div whose id is "d3." If the div is visible, the statement makes it invisible by sliding it up over the course of 3 seconds. If it's invisible, the statement makes it visible by sliding it down over the course of 3 seconds.

```
$("div#d3").toggle(3000);
```

Find a demo for this chapter at:
http://jsfiddle.net/ASmarterWayToLearn/4gsewys5/

Find the interactive coding exercises for this chapter at:
http://www.ASmarterWayToLearn.com/jquery/12.html

13
CHANGE STYLING INLINE

Instead of adding a class that changes element styles as you learned to do in Chapter 2, you can manipulate styling directly. You can style elements inline, like this.

```
$("h2.important").css("color", "red");
```

The code above selects all h2 headings of the class "important" and makes the text color red.

Things to notice:

- After the dot, you write **css**.

- Next come parentheses. Inside them are the property—in this case **"color"**—and the value you specify for that property—in this case **"red."** Both the property and its value are enclosed in quotation marks. A comma comes after the property.

You can specify more than one style property:

```
$("h2.important").css({
  "font-family": "'Times New Roman', Times, serif",
  "font-size": "1.3em",
  "color": "red"
});
```

The code above specifies a font family, a size, and a color for all h2 headings of the "important" class.

Things to notice:

- After **css** comes an opening parenthesis and an opening curly bracket.

- The CSS statements are indented two spaces.

- The property is in quotation marks and is followed by a colon.

- The value of the property is also in quotation marks.

- Each CSS statement, except for the last, ends in a comma.

- The open parenthesis and bracket that end the first line are closed on the last line. A semicolon completes it.

Find a demo for this chapter at:

http://jsfiddle.net/ASmarterWayToLearn/nx3ntL0r/

Find the interactive coding exercises for this chapter at:

http://www.ASmarterWayToLearn.com/jquery/13.html

14
THIS

When the user mouses over a paragraph of grey text, its color changes to black.

The CSS styling might look like this:

```
p.color_changeable {
  color: grey;
}
```

I'm going to use the inline method to change the text color:

```
$("p.color_changeable").on("mouseover", function() {
  $("p.color_changeable").css("color", "black");
});
```

When the user clicks the paragraph, the text turns from grey to black.

Suppose you have more than one paragraph of the class "color_changeable." Then, when the user clicks a paragraph, *all* the paragraphs of that class turn black. If you want only the paragraph clicked to turn black, you code this:

```
$("p.color_changeable").on("mouseover", function() {
  $(this).css("color", "black");
});
```

this refers to the particular paragraph that was clicked. Only **this** paragraph turns black. All the other paragraphs of the class "color_changeable" remain grey.

Note that **this** is not enclosed in quotation marks.

Find a demo for this chapter at:

http://jsfiddle.net/ASmarterWayToLearn/kan9xrp9/

Find the interactive coding exercises for this chapter at:

http://www.ASmarterWayToLearn.com/jquery/14.html

15
SELECT MULTIPLE ELEMENTS

You can target as many elements as you want in a single statement. For example, the following code colors four types of elements light grey:

```
$("h3, p.not_so_important, div#fine_print,
ul#things_to_check li.secondary").css("color",
"#999");
```

The four types of elements targeted here are:

- h3 headings

- paragraphs of the class "not_so_important"

- a div with the id "fine_print."

- all list items of the class "secondary" that are in a list with an id of "things_to_check"

Note that all four CSS selectors are enclosed within a single set of quotation marks and parentheses. They're separated by a comma followed by a space.

Find a demo for this chapter at:

http://jsfiddle.net/ASmarterWayToLearn/jdouezc5/

Find the interactive coding exercises for this chapter at:

http://www.ASmarterWayToLearn.com/jquery/15.html

16
AN ALTERNATIVE FOR SELECTING MULTIPLE ELEMENTS

In the last chapter I selected four different types of elements by writing...

```
$("h3, p.not_so_important, div#fine_print,
ul#things_to_check").css("color", "#999");
```

The following code accomplishes the same thing, but a bit faster (for the processor, not for you):

```
$("h3").add("p.not_so_important").add("div#fine_print
).add("ul#things_to_check").css("color", "#999");
```

The first target—"h3"—is handled normally. Additional targets are handled with **.add("[selector]")**.

Find a demo for this chapter at:
http://jsfiddle.net/ASmarterWayToLearn/7kztnktf/

Find the interactive coding exercises for this chapter at:
http://www.ASmarterWayToLearn.com/jquery/16.html

17
REPLACE AN ID

In Chapter 2, you learned how to add a class to an element. But suppose it's an id rather than a class? You can't *add* an id, because an element can have only one id. But you can *replace* an element's original id with a new one. You use the **attr()** method.

The attr() method assigns an attribute-value pair to an element—the height of an image, the width of a div, the URL of an href, the id of a paragraph. Wherever you see **[something] = [something else]** in an HTML tag, that's an attribute-value pair. And you can make new attribute-value assignments in jQuery.

When the user mouses over the div with an id of "d1," jQuery says it's now to have an id (the attribute) of "d2" (the value). Now its id is "d2," and no longer "d1."

```
$("div#d1").on("mouseover", function() {
  $(this).attr("id", "d2");
});
```

You can use the same method to replace all of an element's classes.

```
$("img.small").on("mouseover", function() {
  $(this).attr("class", "big");
});
```

When the user mouses over any image of the class "small," jQuery replaces all of its class with the class "big."

Note that if an element originally has more than one class, the code above will replace *all* of the element's classes with the new one.

You can assign more than one class to an element:

```
$("img.small").on("mouseover", function() {
  $(this).attr("class", "big splashy");
});
```

Find a demo for this chapter at:
http://jsfiddle.net/ASmarterWayToLearn/ayztekqn/
Find the interactive coding exercises for this chapter at:
http://www.ASmarterWayToLearn.com/jquery/17.html

18
REMOVE THINGS

In Chapter 1 you made all the images vanish using the **hide()** method. Alternatively, you can **remove()** elements. The following code removes all the images on the page:

```
$("img").remove();
```

The following code removes all paragraphs of the class "expendable."

```
$("p.expendable").remove();
```

The code above removes both the opening and closing paragraph tags and everything inside them.

To leave the opening and closing paragraph tags in place but delete all their content, write:

```
$("p.customizable").empty();
```

Originally, if you have three paragraphs like this...

```
<p class="customizable">Hello World!</p>
<p class="customizable">Goodbye World!</p>
<p class="customizable">Hello Mars!</p>
```

...the **empty()** method leaves you with this:

```
<p></p>
<p></p>
<p></p>
```

Later, if you wanted to, you could fill the empty paragraphs with new content using the **text()** or **html()** methods you learned in Chapter 4.

Find a demo for this chapter at:
http://jsfiddle.net/ASmarterWayToLearn/gjtxn3rs/
Find the interactive coding exercises for this chapter at:
http://www.ASmarterWayToLearn.com/jquery/18.html

19
TOGGLE A CLASS

The user clicks a button to hide all the images on the page. She clicks it again to unhide the images.

Begin by creating a button with an id:

```
<button id="toggle_images">Hide/Unhide
Images</button>
```

Create a class that makes elements invisible:

```
.invisible {
  display: none;
}
```

Create an event:

```
$("button#toggle_images").on("click", function() {
  $("img").toggleClass("invisible");
});
```

The **toggleClass()** method adds the class if the element doesn't have the class and removes the class if the element *does* have the class. Since the class in this example hides elements, the elements disappear when the class is added and reappear when it's removed.

I can make the user interface a little slicker by toggling the button text. Initially, it says "Hide images." After images are hidden, it says, "Show images."

```
$("button#toggle_images").on("click", function() {
  $("img").toggleClass("invisible");
  if ($("button#toggle_images").text() === "Hide
images") {
    $("button#toggle_images").text("Show images");
  }
  else {
    $("button#toggle_images").text("Hide images");
  }
});
```

I won't test you on the example code above that toggles button text since it contains JavaScript conditionals. You can learn more about these *if...else* statements in Chapter 12 of my "A Smarter Way to Learn JavaScript".

Find a demo for this chapter at:
http://jsfiddle.net/ASmarterWayToLearn/nsqw9v87/
Find the interactive coding exercises for this chapter at:
http://www.ASmarterWayToLearn.com/jquery/19.html

20
REPLACE THINGS

Suppose you have a paragraph that says "Hello, Dude." Your page has learned, through a form that the user has filled out, that the current user is Australian. You want to replace the paragraph text, "Hello, Dude," with "G'day, Mate." The id of the paragraph is "greeting."

Here's the code that you might *think* would do the job:

```
$("p#greeting").replaceWith("G'day, Mate.");
```

But that's not going to give you the result you want, because the **replaceWith()** method doesn't replace just the *contents* of an element with new contents. It replaces the *element itself* and *everything* inside it. So if the original HTML you're operating on is this...

```
<p id="greeting" class="american"><em>Hello,
Dude</em></p>
```

...the jQuery statement above would leave you with this:

Gday, Mate

The paragraph tags would be gone. The id would be

gone. The class would be gone. And the italics would be gone. So to preserve all the markup and just change the text, you'd write:

```
$("p#greeting").replaceWith("<p id='greeting' class='australian'><em>G'day, Mate.</em></p>");
```

Notice that I enclosed the id and class names in single quotes, since the whole replacement string is enclosed in double quotes.

Find a demo for this chapter at:
http://jsfiddle.net/ASmarterWayToLearn/n23kwca6/
Find the interactive coding exercises for this chapter at:
http://www.ASmarterWayToLearn.com/jquery/20.html

21
ANOTHER WAY TO REPLACE

In the last chapter you learned to replace an element and all its content. You selected the element by id. But you can also select elements by their contents.

On your page you have an h3 heading "Hello, Dude." When the user is an Australian, you want to replace that text with "G'day, Mate."

First you target any headings that contain the text you want to replace...

```
$("h3:contains('Hello, Dude.')")...
```

The code above selects any h3 headings that contain "Hello, Dude."

The second part of the statement is something you learned in Chapter 4. It's the method that replaces the original content within the element with new text:

```
$("h3:contains('Hello, Dude.')").text("G'day,
Mate.");
```

If, instead of replacing the content of an element with text only, you want to replace the element and all its content including HMTL tags, you'd use the **html()** method instead:

```
$("h3:contains('Hello,
Dude.')").html("<h3><em>G'day,</em> Mate.</h3>");
```

The punctuation for this selector can be confusing. I'll break it down for you.

The two layers of wrapping are familiar to you.

```
$("h3:contains('Hello, Dude.')")
```

The CSS selector name is wrapped in quotation marks, and then in parentheses. So far, nothing new.

Instead of a **#** that would select an id, you write a colon.

Then comes the keyword **contains**.

Finally, there's the text you're looking for. It's wrapped in *single* quotes, and then in its own set of parentheses. Single quotes are necessary, because of the outer double quotes.

```
$("h3:contains('Hello, Dude.')")
```

The replacement text is enclosed in double quote,

because there are no outer double quotes.

```
$("h3:contains('Hello, Dude.')").text("G'day,
Mate.");
```

This isn't the easiest syntax to master. If you need to do the exercises for this chapter twice or even three times before you get the hang of it, don't blame yourself. Blame jQuery.

This type of selector can be used to accomplish any number of things. For example, suppose you want to add the class "important" to any paragraph that contains the text "WARNING!" This is the code:

```
$("p:contains('WARNING!')").addClass("important");
```

Find a demo for this chapter at:
http://jsfiddle.net/ASmarterWayToLearn/xfzpuaya/1/
Find the interactive coding exercises for this chapter at:
http://www.ASmarterWayToLearn.com/jquery/21.html

22
VARIABLES IN JQUERY

Let's say you've coded a paragraph that has the id "slider". The paragraph will slide into view *a la* Chapter 11. Then, when the user clicks anywhere on the page, the paragraph will slide up and out of view.

First, you hide it:

```
$("p#slider").hide();
```

Then you slide it, at 2.5-second speed:

```
$("p#slider").slideDown(2500);
```

Then you watch for a click. Since the selector is **$("body")**, which encloses all the elements on the page, the user can click anywhere on the page to trigger the function.

```
$("body").on("click", function() {
  $("p#slider").slideUp();
});
```

The whole sequence looks like this:

```
$("p#slider").hide();
$("p#slider").slideDown(2500);
$("body").on("click", function() {
  $("p#slider").slideUp();
});
```

In the code above, I've highlighted the selector $("p#slider") to point out the repetition. How to make things less cumbersome: Load the selector into a JavaScript variable, then substitute the variable for the selector in the subsequent jQuery statements. The longer and more complicated a selector, the more appealing this approach will be:

```
var tgt = $("p#slider");
tgt.hide();
tgt.slideDown(2500);
$("body").on("click", function() {
  tgt.slideUp();
});
```

Again, notice that the variable declaration in the first line begins with the keyword **var**. It says: "I declare the following to be a variable."

Some coders would start the variable name with a dollar sign, to signal to human readers that the variable refers to a jQuery object—in this case, $("p#slider"). They'd write **$tgt** instead of **tgt**. But jQuery doesn't require this, and I won't, either.

You can also use plain, non-jQuery JavaScript variables in jQuery. The following code stores the number 2500 in the variable **slide_speed**, then specifies **slide_speed** as the **slideDown** speed.

```
var tgt = "p#slider";
var slide_speed = 2500;
$(tgt).hide();
$(tgt).slideDown(slide_speed);
$("body").on("click", function() {
  $(tgt).slideUp();
});
```

You can name variables anything you like, as long as you follow JavaScript's variable-naming rules. I'll cover the rules in the next chapter.

Find a demo for this chapter at:
http://jsfiddle.net/ASmarterWayToLearn/7r1y486f/
Find the interactive coding exercises for this chapter at:
http://www.ASmarterWayToLearn.com/jquery/22.html

23
VARIABLE NAMES LEGAL AND ILLEGAL

A variable name...

- Can't be enclosed in quotation marks.

- Can't contain any spaces.

- Can contain only letters, numbers, dollar signs, and underscores.

- Can't *start* with a number.

- Capital letters are fine, but be careful. Variable names are case sensitive. A **rose** is not a **Rose**. If you assign the string "Floribundas" to the variable **rose**, and then ask JavaScript for the value assigned to **Rose**, you'll come up empty.

A variable name can't be any of JavaScript's reserved words or keywords—the special words that act as programming instructions, like **alert** and **var**. Here's a list of reserved words that can't be used as variable names:

abstract	final	public
alert	finally	return
as	float	short
boolean	for	static
break	function	super)
byte	goto	switch
case	if	synchronize
catch	implements	d
char	import	this
class	in	throw
continue	instanceof	throws
const	int	transient
debugger	interface	true
default	is	try
delete	long	typeof
do	namespace	use
double	native	var
else	new	void
enum	null	volatile
export	package	while
extends	private	with
false	protected	

Though a variable name can't be any of JavaScript's keywords, it can *contain* keywords. For example, **userAlert** and **myVar** are legal.

- I teach the camelCase naming convention. Why "camelCase"? Because there is a hump or two (or three or more) in the middle if the name is formed by more than one word. A camelCase name begins in lower case. If there's more than one word in the name, each subsequent word gets an initial cap, creating a hump. If you form a variable name with only one word, like response, there's no hump. It's a camel that's out of food. Please adopt the camelCase convention. It'll make your variable names more readable, and you'll be less likely to get variable names mixed up.

Examples:

```
userResponse
userResponseTime
userResponseTimeLimit
response
```

- Make your variable names descriptive, so it's easier to figure out what your code means when you or someone else comes back to it three weeks or a year from now. Generally, **userName** is better than **x**, and **faveBreed** is better than **favBrd**, though the shorter names are perfectly legal. You do have to balance readability with conciseness, though. **bestSupportingActressInADramaOrComedy** is a model of clarity, but may be too much for most of us to type or read. I'd shorten it.

Find the interactive coding exercises for this chapter at:

http://www.ASmarterWayToLearn.com/jquery/23.html

24
PERSONALIZE A HEADING

Let's put together some things you already know to do something new.

You ask the user to enter her first and last names in a form with an id of "userName." When the user submits the form, you store her entries in two variables.

```
$("form#userName").on("submit", function() {
    var first_name = $("input#firstName").val();
    var last_name = $("input#lastName").val();
});
```

There's nothing new here.

- You select the form with an id of "userName":
  `$("form#userName")`

- You watch for the submit event:
  `.on("submit"`

- When it happens, you execute a function:
  `, function() {`

- The function stores the user's entries in variables:
  `var first_name =`
  `$("input#firstName").val();`
  `var last_name =`
  `$("input#lastName").val();`

Your HTML contains an empty h4 heading with an id:

```
<h4 id="personalizedQuote"></h4>
```

The function fills this heading with personalized text:

```
$("form#userName").on("submit", function() {
  var first_name = $("input#firstName").val();
  var last_name = $("input#lastName").val();
  $("h4#personalizedQuote").text("Personal Quote for
" + first_name + " " + last_name);
});
```

The text is a combination—a *concatenation* in

programming terms—of four pieces:

1. A text segment: **"Personal Quote for "**

2. The first variable: **first_name**

3. A space: **"   "**

4. The second variable: **last_name**

The plus sign between pieces strings them together to form...

Personal Quote for Dorothy Parker

...if "Dorothy" and "Parker" were entered as the user's names.

Find a demo for this chapter at:
http://jsfiddle.net/ASmarterWayToLearn/ankf042n/
Find the interactive coding exercises for this chapter at:
http://www.ASmarterWayToLearn.com/jquery/24.html

25
ADD HTML TO EXISTING TEXT

Suppose you want to bold some text in response to a user's action. Do it by combining two methods you already know: **html()** and **text()**.

The paragraph that you're going to bold has an id of "important."

Begin by storing the selector in a variable:

```
var okToBold = $("p#important");
```

Start with the variable...

```
okToBold
```

...add the **html()** method...

```
okToBold.html(
```

...add the opening tags...

```
okToBold.html("<p id='important'><strong>"
```

Concatenate with the existing text...

```
okToBold.html("<p id='important'><strong>" +
okToBold.text()
```

Add the closing tags.

```
okToBold.html(""<p id='important'><strong>" +
okToBold.text() + "</strong></p>");
```

The text of the paragraph now displays bold.

Find a demo for this chapter at:
http://jsfiddle.net/ASmarterWayToLearn/1o52sf3z/
Find the interactive coding exercises for this chapter at:
http://www.ASmarterWayToLearn.com/jquery/25.html

26
CHAINING

In Chapter 11 I first hid a paragraph, then slid it into view. This was the code:

```
$("p#slider").hide();
$("p#slider").slideDown(2500);
```

A more concise way to do this is to *chain* the two methods in a single statement:

```
$("p#slider").hide().slideDown(2500);
```

This way, you only need to write the selector once.

Note that each method is separated from the previous one by a dot.

Here's a chain that removes a class, adds a new class, and then changes the color using the inline method:

```
$("h3#products).removeClass("subtle").addClass("drama
tic").css("color", "#ccc");
```

It reads almost like a sentence:

"Select the h3 heading that has the id 'products,' remove

the class 'subtle,' add the class 'dramatic,' and make the color grey."

Find a demo for this chapter at:
http://jsfiddle.net/ASmarterWayToLearn/x2wntfee/
Find the interactive coding exercises for this chapter at:
http://www.ASmarterWayToLearn.com/jquery/26.html

27
ADDING JQUERY TO YOUR PAGE

Don't try to memorize anything in this chapter. You won't be tested on it. The online exercises for this chapter will review things you learned in the first 26 chapters.

jQuery is nothing but a big JavaScript file, with JavaScript's **.js** extension. Your HTML document can link to a jQuery file you've stored on your hard drive, or it can link to a remote jQuery file stored on a server at a Content Delivery Network (CDN), like the one Google maintains. (See below.)

To download the file to your hard drive, go to https://jquery.com/download/. You can choose a *compressed production* version or *uncompressed development* version. If you just want the functionality of jQuery, choose a compressed production version. If you want to look at the JavaScript under the hood and see how jQuery is constructed, choose an uncompressed development version. Of course, you can download both if you wish.

You can also choose between version 1.*x.y* and version 2.*x.y*. Generation 2 doesn't support Internet Explorer 6, 7, or 8.

You want everything on the page to load before jQuery.

Otherwise, jQuery may start looking for something on the page that isn't there yet. The usual way to keep jQuery from jumping the gun is to insert its tag just before the closing **</body>** tag. Let's say your jQuery file is on your hard drive, in the subdirectory "scripts" under the directory where your HMTL file is stored. To link your HTML file to it, you write:

```
    <script src="scripts/jquery-2.1.3.min[or whatever
the latest version is].js">
    </script>
```

So you have two separate sets of opening and closing **<script>** and **</script>** tags:

```
<script src="scripts/jquery-2.1.3.min[or whatever the
latest version is].js">
</script>
<script>
  [Your jQuery and JavaScript code goes here.]
</script>
```

In most situations, the preferred way to get the jQuery file is to link to a CDN like Google, placing the link just above your closing **</body>** tag:

```
<script src=
"https://ajax.googleapis.com/ajax/libs/jquery/1.11.2[
or whatever the latest version is]/jquery.min.js">
</script>
```

Below the jQuery link, you write your jQuery code, along

with any JavaScript code, inside separate opening and closing **<script>** tags:

```
<script>
  [Your jQuery and JavaScript code goes here.]
</script>
```

Alternatively, you can put your jQuery code, as well as any JavaScript code, in a separate JavaScript file, with a **js** extension. In this case, place a link to your file after the link to the jQuery file. For example:

```
<script
src="https://ajax.googleapis.com/ajax/libs/jquery/1.1
1.2[or whatever the latest version
is]/jquery.min.js"></script>
<script src="my_scripts[or whatever you name
it].js"></script>
```

Find interactive coding exercises at:

http://www.ASmarterWayToLearn.com/jquery/27.html

28
DOCUMENT.READY

Don't try to memorize anything in this chapter. You won't be tested on it. The online exercises for this chapter will review things you learned in the first 27 chapters.

In the last chapter, you learned to place the link to your jQuery file just above the closing **</body>** tag, to prevent jQuery code from jumping the gun on HTML page elements that haven't had a chance to load. Coders used to be taught to place script links up high in the head section of an HTML document. Some of these coders are still around. So, to guard against the possibility that one of them will come along at some point and move a properly placed link up into a location that might cause mischief, defensive coders wrap their jQuery code in a *self-invoking, anonymous function* that holds jQuery at bay until the whole page is loaded—that is, until the **document** is **ready**.

If you spend any time around jQuery code, you're going to see it. You may even choose to use it yourself. So I want you to be familiar with it. In the following code, the highlighted portions comprise the function that wraps around a jQuery click event that you learned in Chapter 9. The usual indentation conventions apply.

```
$(document).ready(function() {
  $("button#b1").on("click", function() {
    $("img").hide();
  });
});
```

Find interactive coding exercises at:

http://www.ASmarterWayToLearn.com/jquery/28.html

29
ADD SOMETHING AT THE END

You can tack things onto the end of other things. For example, suppose this markup appears in your HTML document:

```
<ul id="vegetables">
  <li id="i1">lettuce</li>
  <li id="i2">celery</li>
  <li id="i3">carrots</li>
</ul>
```

The markup above displays this on the page:

- lettuce

- celery

- carrots

The following code adds a new item, "rutabaga," to the list:

```
$("ul#vegetables").append("<li>rutabagas</li>");
```

Now this is displayed on the page:

- lettuce

- celery

- carrots

- rutabagas

As you can see from the example, you can append HTML markup as well as text. In the example above, **<li>** and **</li>** are included in the append. It's necessary to include these tags if you want to include rutabagas as a list item, rather than just text. If, omitting the tags, you write...

```
$("ul#vegetables").append("rutabagas");
```

...you get this:

- lettuce

- celery

- carrots

rutabagas

Of course, you can append nothing but text when you want to. Suppose you want to add some text to the first list item, which has an id of "i1." Here's the code:

```
$("li#i1").append(", Romaine");
```

The page displays this:

- lettuce, Romaine

- celery

- carrots

Find a demo for this chapter at:
http://jsfiddle.net/ASmarterWayToLearn/y03t5q7v/

Find the interactive coding exercises for this chapter at:
http://www.ASmarterWayToLearn.com/jquery/29.html

30
ADD SOMETHING AT THE BEGINNING

You can tack things onto the beginning of other things. For example, suppose this markup appears in your HTML document:

```
<div id="d1">
  <p id="p1">Paragraph 1</p>
  <p id="p2">Paragraph 2</p>
  <p id="p3">Paragraph 3</p>
</div>
```

This is how it displays on the page:

Paragraph 1

Paragraph 2

Paragraph 3

The following code places an h2 heading at the beginning of the div, above the first paragraph...

```
$("div#d1").prepend("<h2>These are three important
paragraphs.</h2>");
```

So now this displays on the page:

These are three important paragraphs.

Paragraph 1

Paragraph 2

Paragraph 3

You can also use the **prepend()** method to add text only—without HTML markup—to the beginning of something. For example, you could add some text to the beginning of the second paragraph:

```
$("div#p2").prepend("Be sure to read this important
information carefully: ");
```

This displays:

Paragraph 1

Be sure to read this information carefully:

Paragraph 2

Paragraph 3

Find a demo for this chapter at:
http://jsfiddle.net/ASmarterWayToLearn/ko1zkfd3/
Find the interactive coding exercises for this chapter at:
http://www.ASmarterWayToLearn.com/jquery/30.html

31
INSERT SOMETHING AFTER
SOMETHING ELSE

In Chapters 29 and 30, you learned how to add a new paragraph to a div, a new item to a list, and so on, using the **append()** and **prepend()** methods. For example, you selected an unordered list, and said, "Add a new list item **<li>** to the end (or beginning) of the list **<ul>**."

Another way to add something new is to select, for example, a list item, and say, "Insert a new list item **<li>** after the selected list item **<li>**." For example, suppose you have this HTML markup:

```
<ul>
   <li id="i1">Apples</li>
   <li id="i2">Oranges</li>
   <li id="i3">Bananas</li>
</ul>
```

The markup produces this:

- Apples

- Oranges

- Bananas

You want to add a new list item, "Grapefruit," after "Oranges." You write:

```
$("li#i2").after("<li>Grapefruit</li>");
```

The result:

- Apples

- Oranges

- Grapefruit

- Bananas

Things to notice:

- The statement begins by selecting the element *after which* the new item will be inserted: `$("li#i2")`

- Next comes the dot and the method: `.after(`

- Finally, the content that is to be inserted. It's enclosed in quotation marks, with a closing parenthesis and semicolon: `"<li>Grapefruit</li>");`

Find a demo for this chapter at:
http://jsfiddle.net/ASmarterWayToLearn/f7tnw6bb/
Find the interactive coding exercises for this chapter at:
http://www.ASmarterWayToLearn.com/jquery/31.html

32
INSERT SOMETHING BEFORE SOMETHING ELSE

You have some images of cute animals. You've assigned all of the images the class "cute." Here's one of them:

You want to insert an h3 heading above all the images of this class. This is the code:

```
$("img.cute").before("<h3>Is this cute or
what?</h3>");
```

The result:

Is this cute or what?

Find a demo for this chapter at:

http://jsfiddle.net/ASmarterWayToLearn/phu43xtb/

Find the interactive coding exercises for this chapter at:

http://www.ASmarterWayToLearn.com/jquery/32.html

33
MORE ABOUT CHANGING ATTRIBUTES

Your page includes a thumbnail image of the slow loris. When the user mouses over the thumbnail, the thumbnail turns into a bigger image of the loris. Here's the HTML markup for the thumbnail:

```
<img src="slow_loris_thumbnail.jpg" id="pic4"
alt="slow loris" width="150" height="150">
```

This is the jQuery:

```
$("img#pic4").on("mouseover", function() {
  $(this).attr("src", "slow_loris_full_size.jpg");
});
```

When the user mouses over the thumbnail, the original image source—**slow_loris_thumbnail.jpg**—is replaced by a new image source: **slow_loris_full_size.jpg**.

There are some problems here that we'll solve in the next chapter, but first, I want to go over the syntax once more with you.

- I introduced you to the method, **attr()**, in an earlier chapter. It stands for **attr**ibute.

- The method name is followed by an opening parenthesis. In the example, the first term inside the parenthesis is "src." That's the attribute whose value the statement is going to change. It's in quotation marks.
  ```
  $(this).attr("src"
  ```

- Then comes a comma. It's followed by the second term—what we're changing the value of the attribute *to*. In this case, we're changing it to a different image file. The file name is in quotation marks.
  ```
  $(this).attr("src",
  "slow_loris_full_size.jpg");
  ```

Find a demo for this chapter at:

http://jsfiddle.net/ASmarterWayToLearn/ryfcgcho/

Find the interactive coding exercises for this chapter at:

http://www.ASmarterWayToLearn.com/jquery/33.html

34
REMOVE AN ATTRIBUTE

In the last chapter I showed you how to replace a small picture with a big one when the user mouses over it, by changing the "src" attribute of the first image.

But look at the HTML again.

```
<img src="slow_loris_thumbnail.jpg" id="pic4"
alt="slow loris" width="150" height="150">
```

The new image is four times the size of the original, but in the HTML markup, I've specified width and height attributes of 150 pixels. This means the new image, though bigger, will be scaled down to the same thumbnail size of the original. It'll look exactly like the original thumbnail image.

The best practice would be to change the width and height attributes at the same time as I'm changing the "src" attribute.

```
$("img#pic4").on("mouseover", function() {
  $(this).attr("src",
"slow_loris_full_size.jpg").attr("width",
"600").attr("height", "600");
});
```

Now when the user mouses over the image, the new image replaces it—*and* the width and height attributes change too, to allow the image to display full-size.

If we're going to the trouble to change the width and height attributes, why not just leave the original image in place and blow it up four times using the last part of the code? We could do it, but the quality of the image would suffer. It's okay to reduce the size of an image, but not to blow it up bigger than the original.

Experienced coders usually specify width and height, but you don't absolutely have to. To keep the larger image from scaling down to the dimensions specified in the HTML tag, you could code this:

```
$("img#pic4").on("mouseover", function() {
  $(this).attr("src",
"slow_loris_full_size.jpg").removeAttr("width").remov
eAttr("height");
});
```

The code above solves the resizing problem by removing the width and height specifications altogether. This allows the larger image to display at its full size.

Things to notice:

- **removeAttr** is in camelCase. You must capitalize the **A**.

- Within the parentheses, there is only one term, the name of the attribute to be removed.

Find a demo for this chapter at:

http://jsfiddle.net/ASmarterWayToLearn/26uq71h3/

Find the interactive coding exercises for this chapter at:

http://www.ASmarterWayToLearn.com/jquery/34.html

35

DEALING WITH ID AND CLASS ATTRIBUTES

We've changed the image source of a thumbnail image. We've also changed or removed original width and height attributes. But there's one more potential problem. Here's the original HTML markup that we started with.

```
<img src="slow_loris_thumbnail.jpg" id="pic4"
alt="slow loris" width="150" height="150">
```

If you've associated style characteristics with the id that you don't want to apply to the replacement picture, you need to either remove the id or replace it.

To remove it, as you learned to do in Chapter 34:

```
$("img#pic4").on("mouseover", function() {
  $(this).attr("src",
"slow_loris_full_size.jpg").attr("width",
"600").attr("height", "600").removeAttr("id");
});
```

To replace it, as you learned to do in Chapter 17:

```
$("img#pic4").on("mouseover", function() {
  $(this).attr("src",
"slow_loris_full_size.jpg").attr("width",
"600").attr("height", "600").attr("id", "[name of new
id]");
});
```

And to be clear about classes...

The following code removes all classes from the selected element:

```
$("img#pic4").removeAttr("class");
```

The following code preserves all classes and adds a new class:

```
$("img#pic4").addClass("prominent");
```

The following code replaces all classes with a new class:

```
$("img#pic4").attr("class", "prominent");
```

Find a demo for this chapter at:

http://jsfiddle.net/ASmarterWayToLearn/kvoco1e4/

Find the interactive coding exercises for this chapter at:

http://www.ASmarterWayToLearn.com/jquery/35.html

36

CHANGING ATTRIBUTES:
TWO MORE EXAMPLES

Let's say your page contains a number of links to Amazon:

```
<a href="http://www.amazon.com" class="am"
target="_blank">Amazon</a>
```

For U.K. users, you provide a button that changes the link:

```
<button id="goUK">I live in the U.K.<button>
```

When the user clicks the "I live in the U.K." button, all the links change to the U.K. URL:

```
$("button#goUK").on("click", function() {
  $("a.am").attr("href", "http://www.amazon.co.uk/");

});
```

Suppose you have some textareas, each with 4 rows and 50 columns. You've assigned them the class "expandable." The user can drag the corner to expand them, but for unsophisticated users, you have a button below each one, "Give me more room for my answer." You could write...

```
$("button#moreRoom").on("click", function() {
  $("textarea.expandable").attr("rows",
"8").attr("cols", "100");
});
```

When the user clicks the button, the textarea doubles in both height and width.

Find a demo for this chapter at:
http://jsfiddle.net/ASmarterWayToLearn/j9y38gjw/
Find the interactive coding exercises for this chapter at:
http://www.ASmarterWayToLearn.com/jquery/36.html

37
MAKE A "SHOW MORE" FEATURE

If you shop for books on Amazon—and as an author sustained by Amazon I hope you do—you often see a truncated block of text under the heading "Book Description." Beneath this you see, "Show more," which is clickable. When you click it, the book description expands to full length. Facebook does something similar with its "Trending" column.

Let's make this feature.

Here's the HTML:

```
<p id="ex_1" class="short">A biologist, a chemist,
and a statistician are out hunting. The biologist
shoots at a rabbit and misses five feet to the left.
The chemist shoots, and misses five feet to the
right. The statistician yells, "We got him!"</p>
<a href="javascript:void(0)" id="show_more">Show
more</a></p>
```

The link `<a href="javascript:void(0)"`... doesn't link to anything. But it looks like a link, so the user knows she can click it. I discuss this workaround in Chapter 45 of "A Smarter Way to Learn JavaScript."

In your CSS you shortchange the paragraph on height, so

only the first few lines display.

```
p.short {
  height: 4em;
  overflow: hidden;
}
```

overflow: hidden keeps the full text from breaking out below the paragraph's lower boundary.

You create a second class of paragraph that specifies that the paragraph should be exactly as high as it needs to be to accomodate all the text:

```
p.full_height {
  height: auto;
}
```

When the user clicks "Show more," jQuery adds the "full_height" class to the paragraph, expanding it to show the entire joke:

```
$("a#show_more").on("click", function() {
  $("p.short").addClass("full_height");
});
```

Find a demo for this chapter at:

http://jsfiddle.net/ASmarterWayToLearn/g05vk5bk/

Find the interactive coding exercises for this chapter at:

http://www.ASmarterWayToLearn.com/jquery/37.html

38
ANIMATE AN EXPANSION

In the last chapter, I showed you how to expand a truncated paragraph so all of its text becomes visible. Another approach is to animate the expansion so the user can see it grow. Here's how to do it, using the same elements I used in the last chapter:

```
$("a#show_more").on("click", function() {
  $("p#ex_1").animate({height: "10em"});
});
```

Things to notice:

- The original, truncated height is 4em. The statement above tells the program to let the user see the paragraph expand from the bottom down to a height of 10em.

- The name of the method is **animate**.

- Like all methods, the method is followed by parentheses, but...

- Within the parentheses, the details of the animation are enclosed in curly brackets: **animate({height: "10em"})**

- The attribute *isn't* in quotation marks and is followed by a colon: **animate({height: "10em"})**

- The value of the attribute *is* in quotation marks:

```
animate({height: "10em"})
```

Here's a statement that expands both width and height, using pixels rather than ems as the values:

```
$("a#show_more").on("click", function() {
  $("p#ex_1").animate({width: "250px", height:
"300px"});
});
```

Note that a comma separates the two specifications.

Find a demo for this chapter at:

http://jsfiddle.net/ASmarterWayToLearn/6dtg8mme/

Find the interactive coding exercises for this chapter at:

http://www.ASmarterWayToLearn.com/jquery/38.html

39

FLY SOMETHING IN FROM THE SIDE

You run a website that features pictures of cute animals (what a concept!). When the user first comes to the site, a photo flies in from the left side, coming to rest at its final position in the middle of the screen. This feature is called "Cute animal of the day."

You begin with HTML that looks like this:

```
<div id="daily"><h2>Cute animal<br>of the day:<br>the
slow loris</h2></div>
```

You style the div and the h2 heading this way:

```
div#daily {
  width: 400px;
  height: 269px;
  background-image: url("slow_loris.jpg");
  position: absolute;
  left: -400px;
  top: 250px;
}
div#daily h2 {
  font-family: arial, helvetica, sans-serif;
  font-size: 2em;
  font-weight: bold;
  color: white;
  text-align: center;
  padding: 50px 0 0 150px;
}
```

In the code above, I've highlighted things to notice:

- The image is included in the div as a background-image. The background-image is the same size as the div itself.

- The div is assigned absolute position. For an animation of this kind, the element that you're animating must originally be assigned relative, absolute, or fixed position. It can't have default (static) position. If you aren't clear about the different ways to position elements, see Chapters 64 and 84 of my "A Smarter Way to Learn HTML & CSS."

- The horizontal position is -400px, which means it's positioned so far left, it's not in the window at all. The user can't see it. You start the div out of frame so you can fly it in. I used the width of the image as the negative value. A 400-pixel image that's positioned 400 pixels to the left is out of the picture.

- The vertical position: When I specify **top : 250px** I'm saying the picture is to have an original vertical position 250 pixels from the top of the window. Since, in this example, we aren't changing the vertical spacing in the course of the animation, the picture will fly a straight west-to-east route across the screen at its original altitude of 250 pixels from the top of the window.

- Since the image is a background-image, the heading overlays it. I use padding to position the heading on the right side of the background image. Since the heading is enclosed in the div, it'll fly in *with* the div.

Normally, you'd delay flying in the picture for at least a few seconds after the user arrives at the page. But we won't deal with that just yet. Here's the code for the effect:

```
$("div#daily").animate({left: "15%"});
```

The code above animates the div so it moves from wherever it starts out—in this case out of view on the left—to the position specified within the curly brackets—in this case 15% to the right of the left edge of the window. This probably won't position the picture in the center, just somewhere toward the center. In a later chapter, I'll show you how to animate something so it winds up dead-center.

Things to notice:

- To move the div right you use the keyword **left**. In the code above, the final position is **left** 15%.

- Again, the specification is inside curly brackets: **{left: "15%"}**. As before: The attribute name isn't in quotation marks. It's followed by a colon. The value *is* in quotation marks.

- You could specify the value in pixels.

Find a demo for this chapter at:

http://jsfiddle.net/ASmarterWayToLearn/gwh93fka/

Find the interactive coding exercises for this chapter at:

http://www.ASmarterWayToLearn.com/jquery/39.html

40
FLY IT TO THE CENTER

jQuery lets you measure the user's window so you can bring your flying element to the center, or wherever else you want it in relation to the window's sides.

This statement measures the width of the window and stores the value in the variable **windowWidth**:

```
var windowWidth = $(window).width();
```

The selector is **$(window)**. Note that **window** isn't in quotation marks.

The method is **width()**. If the user is on a laptop with a 1280-pixel-wide screen, 1280 is the number that the method will store in the variable. If the user is on an iPad with a 980-pixel-wide screen, the number would be 980.

So let's rewrite the Cute Animal of the Day animation to bring it to the horizontal center of the screen:

```
var windowWidth = $(window).width();
var imageHorizOffset = ((windowWidth - 400) / 2) +
"px";
$("div#daily").animate({left: imageHorizOffset});
```

This is how it works:

- The first line measures the screen width and stores it in the variable **windowWidth**.

- The second line subtracts the width of the image from the width of the window, then divides the remainder by two. This is the number of pixels to offset the image so it's centered horizontally. The number is concatenated with "px," because jQuery needs it in the **animate()** method. For example: **.animate({left: "300px"})** ... For more information on the parentheses used in the math above, see Chapter 7 of my "A Smarter Way to Learn JavaScript." For an explanation of concatenation, see Chapter 8 of that book. The combination of the number plus "px" is stored in the variable **imageHorizOffset**. If the measured width is, say, 1000 pixels, the value of **imageHorizOffset** is "300px".

- The third line animates the picture, using the variable **imageHorizOffset** to specify the number of pixels. Since it's a variable, it isn't enclosed in quotation marks.

If you wished, you could center an element by specifying the same offset from the right, but I'll stick with specifying it from the left here, and in the exercises.

Find a demo for this chapter at:

http://jsfiddle.net/ASmarterWayToLearn/40j9jow8/

Find the interactive coding exercises for this chapter at:

http://www.ASmarterWayToLearn.com/jquery/40.html

41
ANIMATE TWO MOVES AT ONCE

In the last chapter, I made a picture fly across the screen from left to right, centering itself horizontally. Now, let's do it again, but this time, I want to give it a diagonal flight pattern. It'll start at the upper-left-hand corner and fly down to center itself both horizontally *and* vertically. It'll wind up smack in the middle of the screen.

Look at this code:

```
var windowWidth = $(window).width();
var imageHorizOffset = ((windowWidth - 400) / 2) +
"px";
var windowHeight = $(window).height();
var imageVertOffset = ((windowHeight - 270) / 2) +
"px";
$("div#daily").animate({left: imageHorizOffset});
$("div#daily").animate({top: imageVertOffset});
```

The code above includes the code from the last chapter, but now I'm also measuring the height of the window and dropping the picture down from the top to the vertical center. I subtract 270 from the window's height—270 is the height of the picture—and divide it by 2 to get the vertical offset from the top that will center the picture top-to-bottom.

The code above creates a nice animation. The picture flies left to right, stopping at the horizontal center, then flies down to center itself vertically. But that's not exactly the animation I want. I want the picture to fly *diagonally* from the upper left corner and center itself horizontally and vertically at the same time. So I combine both moves in a single animation:

```
var windowWidth = $(window).width();
var imageHorizOffset = ((windowWidth - 400) / 2) +
"px";
var windowHeight = $(window).height();
var imageVertOffset = ((windowHeight - 270) / 2) +
"px";
$("div#daily").animate({left: imageHorizOffset, top:
imageVertOffset});
```

Now the picture moves down at the same time it moves right.

Note the comma separating the two moves.

You can combine any number of effects in a single animation.

Find a demo for this chapter at:

http://jsfiddle.net/ASmarterWayToLearn/uosqm25z/

Find the interactive coding exercises for this chapter at:

http://www.ASmarterWayToLearn.com/jquery/41.html

42

LET JQUERY MEASURE THE PICTURE

In the code I wrote in the last two chapters, I hard-coded the image dimensions into the instructions:

```
var imageHorizOffset = ((windowWidth - 400) / 2) +
"px";
```

That isn't necessary. Just have jQuery measure the dimensions of the div that encloses the image. The div has the same dimensions as its background-image, the loris. Here's the code:

```
var windowWidth = $(window).width();
var divWidth = $("div#daily").width();
var imageHorizOffset = ((windowWidth - divWidth) / 2)
+ "px";
var windowHeight = $(window).height();
var divHeight = $("div#daily").height();
var imageVertOffset = ((windowHeight - divHeight) /
2) + "px";
$("div#daily").animate({left: imageHorizOffset, top:
imageVertOffset});
```

Find a demo for this chapter at:

http://jsfiddle.net/ASmarterWayToLearn/wwwe19ht/

Find the interactive coding exercises for this chapter at:

http://www.ASmarterWayToLearn.com/jquery/42.html

43
MEASURE EXACTLY WHAT YOU WANT WHEN YOU MEASURE WIDTHS AND HEIGHTS

Sometimes you may want to measure the dimensions of an element without its padding, borders, or margins. At other times, you may want to include one or more of these properties in the measurement.

To measure the width and height of an element *without* padding, borders or margins:

```
var element_only_width = $("[element]").width();
var element_only_height = $("[element]").height();
```

To measure the width and height *including* padding:

```
var element_plus_padding_width =
$("[element]").innerWidth();
var element_plus_padding_height =
$("[element]").innerHeight();
```

To measure the width and height including both padding and border:

```
var element_plus_padding_plus_border_width =
$("[element]").outerWidth();
var element_plus_padding_plus_border_height =
$("[element]").outerHeight();
```

To measure the width and height including padding, border, and margin:

```
var element_plus_everything_width =
$("[element]").outerWidth(true);
var element_plus_everything_height =
$("[element]").outerHeight(true);
```

Find a demo for this chapter at:

http://jsfiddle.net/ASmarterWayToLearn/zqperzaq/

Find the interactive coding exercises for this chapter at:

http://www.ASmarterWayToLearn.com/jquery/43.html

44

FLY SOMETHING BY CHANGING ITS MARGIN

The picture of the loris that flies onto the screen can't stay there. The user needs to be able to make it go away.

So you position a boxed **X** in the top-right corner of the screen. When the user clicks it, the picture disappears.

Let's animate it so the picture flies up and out.

You could write `.animate({top: "-1000px"})`. This value is arbitrary. Just make it big enough to assure that the image will be moved far enough so that it'll be out of the window.

But let's do it a different way this time. jQuery allows you to animate CSS properties. This means you can make something fly away by animating a margin change:

```
$("div#dismiss").on("click", function() {
  $("div#daily").animate({marginTop: "-=1000px"});
});
```

The X that the user clicks on is enclosed in a div with the id "dismiss." When the user clicks, the jQuery animation makes the margin change in smooth increments. It's a negative top margin, so the picture flies up and out of frame.

Things to keep in mind:

- It's **marginTop**, in camelCase, not **margin-top**, as the CSS property is written.

- You write "**-=1000px**".

- You could achieve the same effect by animating the bottom margin with a positive value: **animate({marginBottom: "+=1000px"})**.

- You could use percentages or ems as the values.

Here's a statement that flies an image to the right and down at the same time:

```
$("img#monarch").animate({marginLeft: "+=200px",
marginTop: "+=150px"});
```

Find a demo for this chapter at:
http://jsfiddle.net/ASmarterWayToLearn/9mgw255c/

Find the interactive coding exercises for this chapter at:
http://www.ASmarterWayToLearn.com/jquery/44.html

45
DELAY

It's a good idea to give the user a look at the page for a moment, before flying in the picture of the loris. So I'll add a delay:

```
$("div#daily").delay(3000).animate({left: "15%"});
```

When the page loads, jQuery delays the animation for 3,000 milliseconds (3 seconds). Alternatively, you could specify the delay as "slow" or "fast."

Find a demo for this chapter at:
http://jsfiddle.net/ASmarterWayToLearn/pxyoqr0u/
Find the interactive coding exercises for this chapter at:
http://www.ASmarterWayToLearn.com/jquery/45.html

46
STOP A SLIDE OR ANIMATION

There may be times when you want to stop a slide or animation. For example, you could provide a button that the user clicks when she's had enough of a particular effect. Suppose the button has an id of "stop_it." And suppose you're animating an image with an id of "move_around." This is the code:

```
$("button#stop_it").on("click", function() {
  $("img#move_around").stop();
});
```

Suppose you have a series of animations. For example, a div moves from the left to the horizontal center. Then it moves down to the vertical center. Then it moves down to the lower-right corner. Which parts of the series do you want to stop? Do you want to stop the current animation and allow any subsequent ones to execute? Or do you want to stop the current animation and cancel any that follow?

To stop only the current animation and still allow any subsequent animations to execute, use **stop()**, as in the example above.

To stop the current animation and also cancel any

subsequent animations, write this:

```
$("button#stop_it").on("click", function() {
    $("img#move_around").stop(true);
});
```

To quickly complete the current animation and cancel any subsequent animations, write this:

```
$("button#stop_it").on("click", function() {
    $("img#move_around").stop(true, true);
});
```

Find a demo for this chapter at:

http://jsfiddle.net/ASmarterWayToLearn/utat8x9h/

Find the interactive coding exercises for this chapter at:

http://www.ASmarterWayToLearn.com/jquery/46.html

47
SWAP IMAGES USING TOGGLE()

When the user clicks a thumbnail of an attractive house, the thumbnail is replaced by a larger image of the house.

Begin by creating a class that hides an element:

```
.nowhere_element {
  display: none;
}
```

I'll take a moment to mention the difference between **display: none** and **visibility: hidden**. When you specify **display: none**, the element takes up no space on the page. As far as the layout goes, the element doesn't exist. When you specify **visibility: hidden**, the element is invisible but still takes up space on the page. Nothing else can occupy its space. In this example, I use **display: none**, because I want the two images to change places. When I display the larger image, I want the thumbnail to give up its place on the page.

Initially, the HTML markup displays the thumbnail and hides the larger image:

```
<img id="house_thumb" src="house_200.jpg" alt="house"
width="200" height="150">
<img id="house_big" class="nowhere_element"
src="house_600.jpg" alt="house" width="600"
height="150">
```

When the user clicks the thumbnail, the class is toggled for both images. The first toggle adds the "nowhere_element" class to the thumbnail, which removes the thumbnail from the page. The second toggle removes the "nowhere_element" class from the larger image, placing the larger image onto the page. The thumbnail vacates the page, and is replaced by the larger image:

```
$("img#house_thumb").on("click", function() {
  $(this).toggleClass("nowhere_element");
  $("img#house_big").toggleClass("nowhere_element");
});
```

The following code makes both images clickable, so they can be toggled back and forth. When the thumbnail is clicked, it's replaced by the big picture. When the big picture is clicked, it's replaced by the thumbnail.

```
$("img#house_thumb, img#house_big").on("click",
function() {
   $("img#house_thumb").toggleClass("nowhere_element")
;
   $("img#house_big").toggleClass("nowhere_element");
});
```

Even better, for brevity:

```
$("img#house_thumb, img#house_big").on("click",
function() {
   $("img#house_thumb,
img#house_big").toggleClass("nowhere_element");
});
```

Find a demo for this chapter at:

http://jsfiddle.net/ASmarterWayToLearn/ajx9chre/

Find the interactive coding exercises for this chapter at:

http://www.ASmarterWayToLearn.com/jquery/47.html

48
CHANGE OPACITY

You can make elements appear and disappear by changing their opacity.

An element that has opacity of 0 is transparent. An element that has opacity of 1 is fully visible and hides any element beneath it. An element that has opacity of .5 is translucent. You can specify any level of opacity by choosing from a full range of decimals between 0 and 1.

The following code makes the image disappear:

```
$("img#house_big").css({opacity: 0});
```

The following code makes it appear:

```
$("img#house_big").css({opacity: 1});
```

When the user clicks a thumbnail, you can use opacity to make the thumbnail disappear and the larger image appear. Start by making the larger image invisible:

```
$("img#house_big").css({opacity: 0});
```

Then construct the function:

```
$("img#house_thumb").on("click", function() {
  $(this).css({opacity: 0});
  $("img#house_big").css({opacity: 1});
});
```

This won't achieve quite the effect we want. The larger image will be positioned below the space occupied by the invisible thumbnail. To create the effect of the larger image replacing the thumbnail, you can use relative positioning to move the larger image up. Suppose the thumbnail is 100 pixels high. The following code will do the job:

```
$("img#house_thumb").on("click", function() {
  $(this).css({opacity:0});
  $("img#house_big").css({opacity: 1, position:
"relative", top: "-100px"});
});
```

Find a demo for this chapter at:

http://jsfiddle.net/ASmarterWayToLearn/71zztc8w/

Find the interactive coding exercises for this chapter at:

http://www.ASmarterWayToLearn.com/jquery/48.html

49
GIVE SOMETHING A CHANCE TO FINISH

I'm using some new methods in this chapter. The first is **fadeTo()**. It slowly changes the opacity of an element. The second is the JavaScript method **alert()**. It displays a box with a message in it.

After the thumbnail picture of the house is replaced by the larger image that fades into view, I want to display an alert that says, "Purchase this house for just $3 down using PayPal!" But there's a problem. If I write...

```
$("img#house_thumb").on("click", function() {
  $(this).toggleClass("nowhere_element");
  $("img#house_big").fadeTo(1500, 1);
  alert("Purchase this house for just $3 down using
PayPal!");
});
```

...the alert, which executes almost instantly, displays before the fade, which needs time to do its thing, executes. The alert refers to something that isn't visible yet.

In order to delay the alert until the fade executes, I need to use a *callback function*. This means that I place the alert statement inside a function. The only purpose of the function is to delay execution of the alert until the fade completes:

```
$("img#house_thumb").on("click", function() {
  $(this).toggleClass("nowhere_element");
  $("img#house_big").fadeTo(1500, 1, function() {
    alert("Purchase this house for just $3 down using
PayPal!");
  });
});
```

It may be a familiar pattern to you by now. After the first two terms of the **fadeTo**—the speed and opacity level— you add a third thing, the function wrapper. This is separated from the first two terms by a comma and a space. Inside the wrapper, you place the code that executes—in this example, an alert.

Find a demo for this chapter at:

http://jsfiddle.net/ASmarterWayToLearn/b5q8r2v2/

Find the interactive coding exercises for this chapter at:

http://www.ASmarterWayToLearn.com/jquery/49.html

50
MAKE ANIMATED TABS
PART 1

Here's a vertical menu:

.When the user moves the pointer over one of the icons, the tab changes color and expands:

.This is the styling for the expanded tab:

```
div.full_tab {
  position: fixed;
  width: 300px;
  height: 80px;
  background-color: #cc3366;
  left: -300px;
  z-index: 1;
}
```

Things to notice:

- The position is fixed. An element that animates must have relative, absolute, or fixed position.

- The div is positioned 300 pixels to the left—**left: -300px**. Since 300 pixels is the width of the div, moving it left by that amount places it left of the screen, out of sight.

- The div is assigned a z-index of 1 so that when it moves onto the screen, it'll cover up the small, black, icon-only tab. For information on how z-index works, see Chapter 85 of my "A Smarter Way to Learn HTML & CSS."

This is the styling for the heading in the expanded tab—in this example, "Mail":

```
div.full_tab h2 {
    font-family: arial, helvetica, sans-serif;
    font-size: 40px;
    color: white;
    float: right;
    margin: 19px 20px 0 0;
}
```

Since the heading is within the div, it'll be included in the animation.

Find a demo for this chapter at:

http://jsfiddle.net/ASmarterWayToLearn/9m6gkqjd/

Find the interactive coding exercises for this chapter at:

http://www.ASmarterWayToLearn.com/jquery/50.html

51
MAKE ANIMATED TABS
PART 2

When the user moves the pointer over one of the menu icons, jQuery animates the div, moving it from its hidden position to the left of the screen into its visible, fully extended position. As it moves to the right, it covers up the small, black, icon-only tab.

This is the jQuery that animates the "Mail" tab:

```
$("div#tab_mail").on("mouseenter", function() {
  $("div#mail_tab_full").animate({left: "0"},
"fast");
});
```

Things to notice:

- The event is **mouseenter()**, not, as you might expect, **mouseover()**. I'll explain why in the next chapter.

- Animating the div into the **left: 0** position brings it onto the screen and extends it full-width from the left edge of the screen.

- I've specified "fast" animation. Instead, I could specify "slow." Or I could write a number to specify milliseconds. The animation speed is optional. You can omit it altogether.

- Only **left: "0"** is enclosed in the curly brackets. The speed is within the parentheses but outside the curly brackets. A comma and a space separate it from the curly brackets.

Find a demo for this chapter at:
http://jsfiddle.net/ASmarterWayToLearn/x6hj2npc/
Find the interactive coding exercises for this chapter at:
http://www.ASmarterWayToLearn.com/jquery/51.html

52
MAKE ANIMATED TABS
PART 3

When the user moves the pointer away from the expanded tab or clicks it, the expanded tab needs to go back to where it came from—out of sight to the left of the screen. When it moves back out, the black, icon-only tab becomes visible again. This is the code for the "People" tab:

```
$("div#people_tab_full").on("mouseleave", function()
{
  $(this).animate({left: "-300px"}, "fast");
});
$("div#people_tab_full").on("click", function() {
  $(this).animate({left: "-300px"}, "fast");
  window.location = "people.html"
});
```

There's possibly another surprise for you here. The event in the first line isn't **mouseout**, as you might expect, but **mouseleave**. Why am I using **mouseenter** and **mouseleave** to trigger these animations?

The problem with **mouseover** and **mouseout** is that they do more than we want them to in this case. **mouseover** triggers the function when the pointer is on the div, and then again if the pointer moves onto the heading inside the div. **mouseout** triggers *its* function when the pointer departs from the heading inside the div, and then again when the pointer departs from the div. We want just one animation, not a series of them.

mouseenter tells the program to react when the pointer enters the div, but to disregard it when the pointer moves over anything *inside* the div. **mouseleave** tells the program to react when the pointer departs from the div, but to ignore it when the pointer departs from anything *inside* the div.

Find a demo for this chapter at:

http://jsfiddle.net/ASmarterWayToLearn/9uw1Lq18/

Find the interactive coding exercises for this chapter at:

http://www.ASmarterWayToLearn.com/jquery/52.html

53
MAKE ANIMATED TABS
PART 4

Even though we reduce the number of animations by using **mouseenter** and **mouseleave**, jQuery may not stop at animating just once. So we need to tell it to stop after the first animation:

```
$("div#tab_mail").on("mouseenter", function() {
  $("div#mail_tab_full").stop().animate({left: "0"},
"fast");
});
$("div#people_tab_full").on("mouseleave", function()
{
  $(this).stop().animate({left: "-300px"}, "fast");
});
$("div#people_tab_full").on("click", function() {
  $(this).stop().animate({left: "-300px"}, "fast");
  window.location = "people.html"
});
```

By inserting the **stop()** method before each **animate()** method, I am, in effect, telling jQuery to resist its inclination to animate more than once.

Find the interactive coding exercises for this chapter at:

http://www.ASmarterWayToLearn.com/jquery/53.html

54
SIZE DIVS TO FIT THE WINDOW

Webpages that sell a product or service—landing pages—are often organized into screen-size panels that stack vertically. When the user scrolls down, a new panel comes into view. The panels alternate colors or background images so the user sees that each one is a separate section. As the user scrolls down, she intuitively centers each panel vertically in the window.

jQuery can measure the window and then size the panels to fit. Here's code that does the measuring:

```
var windowWidth = $(window).width();
var windowHeight = $(window).height();
```

In the code above, the dimensions of the window, detected by the methods **width()** and **height()**, are stored in variables. This information is used to size the panels:

```
$("div.fit_to_window").css("width", windowWidth *
.85).css("height", windowHeight);
```

Note that in the code above, I give the div a width that's

85% of the window width. When I right-float the div in CSS, this makes room for a narrow vertical menu on the left.

If the vertical content of the div exceeds the height that you've set, the browser will ignore your height specification and stretch the div beyond what you've specified to fit everything in. To keep this from happening, you can style the div **overflow: hidden** or **overflow: auto**. See chapter 87 of A Smarter Way to Learn HTML & CSS.

For more succinct code, you could condense the three statements above into a single statement:

```
$("div.fit_to_window").css("width", $(window).width()
* .85).css("height", $(window).height());
```

Find the interactive coding exercises for this chapter at:

http://www.ASmarterWayToLearn.com/jquery/54.html

55
SCROLL TO THE NEXT PANEL

In the last chapter, I showed you how to create panels that scale to window size. In this type of page design, developers often include a "Learn more" button in the topmost panel. When the user clicks it, the page automatically scrolls down to the next panel.

Begin by measuring the window height, the way I showed you in the last chapter.

```
var windowHeight = $(window).height();
```

With the window's height stored in the variable, tell jQuery to scroll down by that amount:

```
$("button#read_more").on("click", function() {
  $("body").scrollTop(windowHeight);
});
```

Things to notice:

- The selected element is "body"—the entire page.

- The method name is **scrollTop**.

- The amount to scroll is found in **windowHeight**, the variable where you stored the measurement. In the last chapter, we scaled the panels to match the height of the window. So when the page scrolls down by the window's height, the second panel is revealed.

You could make the code more succinct by combining both statements above:

```
$("button#read_more").on("click", function() {
  $("body").scrollTop($(window).height());
});
```

You specify the number of pixels to scroll, with a number:

```
$("button#read_more").on("click", function() {
  $("body").scrollTop(250);
});
```

Find a demo for this chapter at:

http://jsfiddle.net/ASmarterWayToLearn/h6skc763/

Find the interactive coding exercises for this chapter at:

http://www.ASmarterWayToLearn.com/jquery/55.html

56
ANIMATE THE SCROLL

The code in the last chapter gets the job done, but when the user clicks the "Learn more" button, the scroll doesn't look like a scroll. It looks like a clean jump. The user will get a better sense of what's happening if you animate the scroll so it looks like a scroll. This is the code:

```
$("button#read_more").on("click", function() {
  $("body").animate({scrollTop: windowHeight}, 800);
});
```

The code above combines several things you already know how to do:

- Use the **animate()** method.

- Follow the method with parentheses.

- Enclose curly brackets within the parentheses.

- Within the curly brackets, write the method or property—**scrollTop** in this case— followed by a colon.

- Optionally, add an animation speed—800 in this case—outside the curly brackets and separated from the property by a comma.

Find a demo for this chapter at:
http://jsfiddle.net/ASmarterWayToLearn/kjzw24ng/

Find the interactive coding exercises for this chapter at:
http://www.ASmarterWayToLearn.com/jquery/56.html

57

MONITOR THE SCROLL POSITION

jQuery can monitor scrolling, telling you how far down the page the user has scrolled. We'll use the three-panel layout we've been working with.

First, code an empty paragraph where the scroll information will be displayed:

```
<p id="scroll_position_info"></p>
```

Place it in fixed position so it doesn't scroll off the page. I'll put it over on the left, where I've left room for a vertical menu.

```
p#scroll_position_info {
  position: fixed;
  top: 20%;
  left: 2%;
}
```

Code a jQuery function:

```
$(window).scroll(function() {
  $("p#scroll_position_info").html("We're <strong>" +
$(window).scrollTop() + "</strong> pixels<br>from the
top");
});
```

Here's what happens:

- **$(window).scroll(function() {** watches for scrolling. Every time the page moves up or down in the window, the statement in the next line is triggered.

- **$("p#scroll_position_info").html** tells jQuery where to insert the information about the scroll.

- The information—**("We're " + $(window).scrollTop() + " pixels
from the top")**—is a concatenation of some HTML plus a jQuery selector and method.

- **$(window).scrollTop()** measures, in pixels, how far down the page the user has scrolled.

Find a demo for this chapter at:http://jsfiddle.net/ASmarterWayToLearn/nL1e20h2/

Find the interactive coding exercises for this chapter at:

http://www.ASmarterWayToLearn.com/jquery/57.html

58

MAKE SOMETHING HAPPEN WHEN THE USER SCROLLS

When the user scrolls down to the second window-sized panel, a heading flies down from the top and positions itself near the top of the second panel.

First, position the heading out of sight, above the window:

```
h2#loris_promo {
  position: absolute;
  top: -300px;
  font-family: Verdana, Geneva, sans-serif;
  font-size: 3.5em;
  font-weight: bold;
  color: white;
  margin: 0;
  padding-left: 10%;
}
```

When the user scrolls, measure the height of the first panel:

```
$(window).scroll(function() {
  var firstPanHt = $("div#bl_1").height();
  if ($(window).scrollTop() > firstPanHt / 4) {
    $("h2#loris_promo").animate({top: firstPanHt +
100}, 1000);
  }
});
```

When the user scrolls 1/4 of the way down the first panel, exposing the top quarter of the second panel...

```
$(window).scroll(function() {
  var firstPanHt = $("div#bl_1").height();
  if ($(window).scrollTop() > firstPanHt / 4) {
    $("h2#loris_promo").animate({top: firstPanHt +
100}, 1000);
  }
});
```

...trigger the animation. Fly it down to a position 100 pixels below the bottom of the first panel. This places it near the top of the second panel.

```
$(window).scroll(function() {
  var firstPanHt = $("div#bl_1").height();
  if ($(window).scrollTop() > firstPanHt / 4) {
    $("h2#loris_promo").animate({top: firstPanHt +
100}, 1000);
  }
});
```

Find a demo for this chapter at:

http://jsfiddle.net/ASmarterWayToLearn/8j72ffcq/

Find the interactive coding exercises for this chapter at:

http://www.ASmarterWayToLearn.com/jquery/58.html

59
SELECT BY EVEN OR ODD

You can make tables more readable by shading alternate rows, like this.

Dog	Cat	Cow	Horse
Canine	Feline	Bovine	Equine
Bark	Meow	Moo	Whinny
Omnivore	Omnivore	Herbivore	Herbivore
Puppy	Kitten	Calf	Colt

This is the code to select even rows and color their background-color grey:

```
$("tr:even").css("background-color", "#ccc");
```

Note: Since jQuery begins counting at 0, the heading row at the top is row 0. The row that begins with "Bark" is row 2. The row that begins with "Puppy" is row 4. Normally, the heading row would be shaded, but I've overridden the jQuery with CSS styling for that row.

Alternatively, you could define a **tr** class with a grey background-color, and code it this way:

```
$("tr:even").attr("class", "shaded_row");
```

You can also select odd rows:

```
$("tr:odd").css("background-color", "#ccc");
```

The code above produces this:

Dog	Cat	Cow	Horse
Canine	Feline	Bovine	Equine
Bark	Meow	Moo	Whinny
Omnivore	Omnivore	Herbivore	Herbivore
Puppy	Kitten	Calf	Colt

You can select even or odd rows in a class of tables or in a table with a particular id. The following code selects even rows in a table whose id is "pets".

```
$("table#pets tr:odd").css("background-color",
"#ccc");
```

You can use **even** and **odd** to select the even or odd items in any group—for example, the even or odd divs on the page, the even or odd paragraphs in a div, the even or odd items in a list, etc.

Find a demo for this chapter at:

http://jsfiddle.net/ASmarterWayToLearn/1ja3rxkd/

Find the interactive coding exercises for this chapter at:

http://www.ASmarterWayToLearn.com/jquery/59.html

60
SELECT BY FIRST OR LAST

You can select a first or last element and change it. For example, suppose you want to bump up the size of the first paragraph in the main div. This is the code:

```
$("div#main p:first").css("font-size", "1.5em");
```

You can use **first** and **last** to select the first or last items in any group—for example, the first or last divs on the page, the first or last paragraphs in a div, the first or last items in a list, etc.

The following code selects the last image in the document and animates it to a new position on the page:

```
$("image:last").animate({bottom: "100px", "slow"});
```

The following code selects the first div in the document and adds a class to it:

```
$("div:first").addClass("highlighted");
```

Find a demo for this chapter at:

http://jsfiddle.net/ASmarterWayToLearn/andtjy8a/

Find the interactive coding exercises for this chapter at:

http://www.ASmarterWayToLearn.com/jquery/60.html

61
SELECT BY NEXT

Let's get commercial.

You display three buttons. Each button represents a different deal for the customer.

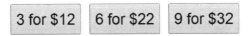

When the customer clicks the first or second button, the next button over pitches a sweeter deal for the user and a bigger sale for you. For example, if she clicks the middle button, choosing 6 for $22, this happens:

The first two buttons have the class "upsell." This is the code:

```
$("button.upsell").on("click", function() {
  $(this).next().html($(this).next().text() +
"<br><span class='urge_more'>Save $2 more by choosing
this deal!</span>");
```

When the user clicks either of the first two buttons, the next element is selected. Using the **html()** method, I concatenate its original text—in this case "9 for $32"—together with some red-colored text telling her she can save $2 more.

What happens if she initially clicks the third button, choosing the most expensive option? As a commercially-minded person, I would be inclined to add a fourth button offering her 12 for $42:

```
$("button#third").on("click", function() {
  $("button#fourth").fadeTo("fast", 1);
});
```

In CSS, the fourth button is originally styled with 0 opacity, so it's invisible. When the third button is clicked, the fourth button fades up into visibility.

In the example, when one of the first two buttons is clicked, **next()** selects the next button. But that's only because the next element in the document happens to be a button. **next()** doesn't select the next element *of the same kind*. It selects the next element of *any* kind. So, for example, if the user clicked a button that triggered a **next()** selection and the next element were an image, the image would be selected.

Find a demo for this chapter at:

http://jsfiddle.net/ASmarterWayToLearn/9xabdh6n/

Find the interactive coding exercises for this chapter at:

http://www.ASmarterWayToLearn.com/jquery/61.html

62
THE DOM

In previous chapters you learned to target elements three different ways:

- By element type—for example **$("p")**, **$("img")**, **$("h2")**—etc.

- By class—for example
  $("p.important"),
  $("img.expandable"),
  $("h2.standout"),
  $("div.product_info"),
  $(".alternate"),
  $(".not_visible")— etc.

- By id—for example **$("p#intro")**,
  $("div#header"),
  $("h2#explanation"),
  $("#addedum"), **$("#hype")**—etc.

There's another way to target elements—by specifying their position in the **DOM**, the **Document Object Model**. The DOM is an organization chart, created automatically by the browser when your webpage loads. All the elements in your HTML document—the tags, the text blocks, the images, the links, the tables, the style attributes, and more—have spots on this organization chart. This means that your jQuery code can get its hands on anything on your webpage, anything at all, just by saying where that thing is on the chart. What's more, your jQuery can add things, move things, or delete things by manipulating the chart. If you wanted to (you wouldn't), you could almost create an entire webpage from scratch using jQuery's DOM methods.

Here's a simplified webpage. I've indented the different levels in the hierarchy. The three top levels of the DOM are always the same for a standard webpage.

1. The document is on the first level.

2. HTML is on the second level.

3. Head and body are co-equals on the third level.

Under each of the top three levels are are more levels.

```
1st level: document
2nd level:    <html>
3rd level:      <head>
4th level:        <title>
5th level:          Simple document
                  </title>
                </head>
3rd level       <body>
4th level         <p>
5th level           There's not much to this.
                  </p>
                </body>
              </html>
```

Here's the same thing, shown as an organization chart.

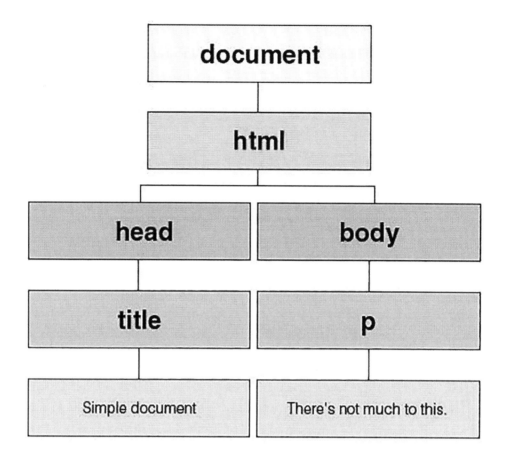

As you can see, every single thing on the webpage is included, even the title text and the paragraph text. Let's make it a little more complicated by adding a div and a second paragraph. Here it is in HTML form.

```
1st level: document
2nd level:    <html>
3rd level:      <head>
4th level:        <title>
5th level:          Simple document
                  </title>
                </head>
3rd level      <body>
4th level        <div>
5th level          <p>
6th level            There's not much to this.
                   </p>
5th level          <p>
6th level            Nor to this.
                   </p>
                 </div>
               </body>
             </html>
```

And in an organization chart...

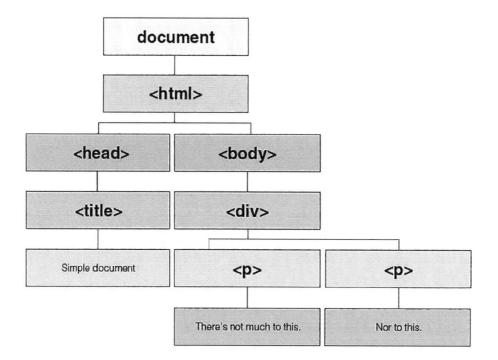

In a company organization chart, each box represents a person. In the DOM organization chart, each box represents a **node**. The HTML page represented above has 11 nodes:

- Document node

- html node

- head and body nodes

- title node

- div node

- two paragraph nodes

- three text nodes, one for the title and one for each of the two paragraphs.

In this particular chart, there are three types of nodes: document, element, and text. The document node is the top level. Element nodes are **<html>**, **<head>**, **<body>**, **<title>**, **<div>**, and **<p>**. Text nodes are the strings that comprise the title and the two paragraphs.

Find the interactive coding exercises for this chapter at: http://www.ASmarterWayToLearn.com/jquery/62.html

63
THE DOM:
PARENTS AND CHILDREN

Can you name the second child of the 44th President of the United States? That would be Sasha. How about the parent (male) of the 43rd President? That's right. It's George.

Welcome to the most fundamental way of designating nodes of the Document Object Model (DOM). You can designate any node of the DOM by saying the node is the xth child of a particular parent. You can also designate a node by saying it's the parent of any child.

Take a look at the simplified html document from the last chapter.

```
1st level: document
2nd level:    <html>
3rd level:      <head>
4th level:        <title>
5th level:          Simple document
                  </title>
                </head>
3rd level       <body>
4th level         <div>
5th level           <p>
6th level              There's not much to this.
                    </p>
5th level           <p>
6th level              Nor to this.
                    </p>
                  </div>
                </body>
              </html>
```

Except for the document node—the node at the top of the hierarchy—each node is enclosed within another node.

- The **\<head\>** and **\<body\>** nodes are enclosed within the **\<html\>** node.

- The **\<div\>** node is enclosed within the **\<body\>** node.

- Two **\<p\>** nodes are enclosed within the **\<div\>** node.

- A text node is enclosed within each of the **\<p\>** nodes.

When a node is enclosed within another node, we say that the enclosed node is a **child** of the node that encloses it. So, for example, the **\<div\>** node is a child of the **\<body\>** node. Conversely, the **\<body\>** node is the **parent** of the **\<div\>** node. Here's the organization chart from the last chapter, showing all the parents and their children.

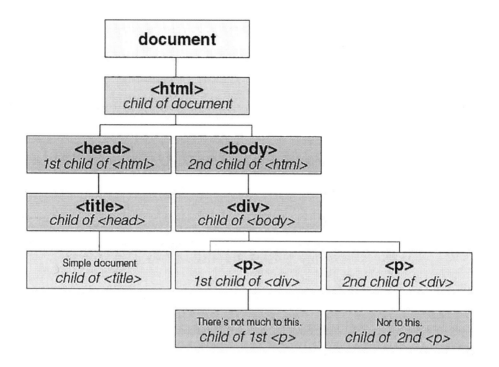

As you can see, **<html>** is the child of the **document**...**<head>** and **<body>** are the children of **<html>**...**<div>** is the child of **<body>**...two **<p>**'s are the children of **<div>**...each text node is the child of a **<p>**. Conversely, the **document** is the parent of **<html>**, **<html>** is the parent of **<head>** and **<body>**, **<head>** is the parent of **<title>**, **<title>** is the parent of a text node, and so on. Nodes with the same parent are known as siblings. So, **<head>** and **<body>** are siblings because **< html>** is the parent of both. The two **<p>**'s are siblings because **<div>** is the parent of both.

Starting at the bottom of the chart, the text "Nor to this." is a child of **<p>**, which is a child of **<div>**, which is a child of **<body>**, which is a child of **<html>**, which is a child of the **document**.

Now look at this markup.

```
<p>This is <em>important</em>!</p>
```

If you made a chart for this paragraph, you might think that all the text inside the paragraph tags is a child of the **<p>** node. But remember, every node that is enclosed by another node is the child of the node that encloses it. Since the text node "important" is enclosed by the element node **<em>**, this particular text node is the child of **<em>**, not **<p>**. The text nodes "This is " and "!" as well as the element node **<em>** are siblings, because they're all enclosed by **<p>**. They're all children of **<p>**.

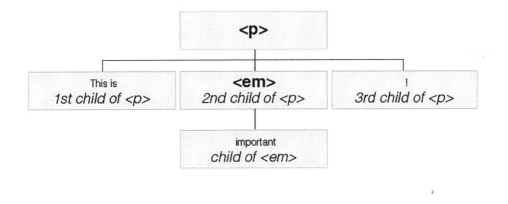

Find the interactive coding exercises for this chapter at:
http://www.ASmarterWayToLearn.com/jquery/63.html

64

SELECT THE FIRST CHILD
OR LAST CHILD

Suppose your DOM structure looks like this:

```
<div>
  <p>Lorem ipsum dolor sit amet, consectetuer
adipiscing elit. Integer tincidunt.</p>
  <p>Aenean commodo ligula eget dolor. Aenean
massa.</p>
  <p>Donec quam felis, ultricies nec, pellentesque
eu, pretium quis, sem.</p>
</div>
<div>
  <p>Nulla consequat massa quis enim. Donec pede
justo, fringilla vel, aliquet nec, vulputate eget,
arcu.</p>
  <p>In enim justo, rhoncus ut, imperdiet a,
venenatis vitae, justo. Nullam dictum felis eu pede
mollis pretium.</p>
</div>
<div>
  <p>Cum sociis natoque penatibus et magnis dis
parturient montes, nascetur ridiculus mus.</p>
  <p>Cras dapibus. Vivamus elementum semper nisi.
Aenean vulputate eleifend tellus.</p>
  <p>Aenean leo ligula, porttitor eu, consequat
vitae, eleifend ac, enim.</p>
  <p>Aliquam lorem ante, dapibus in, viverra quis,
feugiat a, tellus. Phasellus viverra nulla ut metus
varius laoreet. Quisque rutrum.</p>
</div>
```

That's three divs, each containing nothing but paragraphs. You want to increase the font-size of the first paragraph in each div.

For the purposes of this example, I'm going to assume that all paragraphs on the page are the same font-size to begin with.

Since we're assuming all paragraphs share the same font-size, we can measure any of them to get the "normal" font-size. The following code arbitrarily selects the first paragraph on the page as a sample paragraph, and measures its font-size:

```
var normal_size = $("p:first").css("font-size");
```

The original paragraph font-size is now stored in the variable **normal_size**. But there's a complication. In my CSS file, I specified a font-size of 1.25em for paragraphs. jQuery translates that into 20 pixels, which is fine. But the value stored in **normal_size** isn't 20. It's "20px." I want to multiply it by 1.5 to enlarge the first paragraph in each div, but the program balks if I try to multiply "20px" by another number. The "px" part of it means the program doesn't see it as a number and so can't multiply it. So I have to lop off "px," leaving just "20." Then the program will be able to do multiplication on it. To slice off "px," I use the **slice()** method, explained in Chapter 22 of my "A Smarter Way to Learn JavaScript."

```
var increased_size = normal_size.slice(0,
normal_size.length - 2) * 1.5;
```

The Javascript statement above slices off "px," leaving just "20." Then it multiplies by 1.5, getting "30." This number is stored in the variable **increased_size**. That's going to be the new size for every paragraph that is the first child in every div.

Now I code this:

```
$("p:first-child").css("font-size", increased_size +
"px");
```

$("p:first-child") selects every paragraph that is a first child of a parent. So, for example, if you have three divs in the document that have the structure I showed you at the beginning of this chapter, the code above selects the first paragraph in each of those divs.

When the code above executes, the font-size of each targeted paragraph is increased 50%.

To select the last child instead of the first child, write **$("*[element type]*:last-child")**. For example, **$("img:last-child")** selects all images that are the last child of any parent.

Any type of element that's a child of something else—which is to say *any* type of element except document—can be selected this way. You can't select the document this way, because it isn't the child of anything.

Find a demo for this chapter at:

http://jsfiddle.net/ASmarterWayToLearn/vmemrvft/

Find the interactive coding exercises for this chapter at:

http://www.ASmarterWayToLearn.com/jquery/64.html

65
SELECT THE FIRST OR LAST CHILD OF A TYPE

In the last chapter, my jQuery code increased the size of every paragraph that is a first child of a parent. But if the DOM structure had been different, it wouldn't have worked the way I wanted it to. What if one of the divs starts off with a heading rather than a paragraph?—

```
<div>
  <h2>Please take the statements below with a grain
of salt.</h2>
  <p>Lorem ipsum dolor sit amet, consectetuer
adipiscing elit. Integer tincidunt.</p>
  <p>Aenean commodo ligula eget dolor. Aenean
massa.</p>
  <p>Donec quam felis, ultricies nec, pellentesque
eu, pretium quis, sem.</p>
</div>
```

I want to increase the font-size of every first paragraph in each div, but the selector $("p:first-child") won't do that in the div above, because the first paragraph isn't the first child of the div. The h2 heading is. The first paragraph is the *second* child of the div. So I need to be clearer about what I want. I want to say, "Select the first child *that's a paragraph.*"

```
$("p:first-of-type").css("font-size",
increased_size);
```

Now, whether the first *paragraph* in the div is the first *child* or not, I've targeted it.

You can also target the last paragraph of a parent by writing `$("p:last-of-type")`.

You can use this type of selector with any type of element that has a parent, including divs, images, spans, lists, headings, tables, etc.

Find a demo for this chapter at:

http://jsfiddle.net/ASmarterWayToLearn/hxhwh1hx/

Find the interactive coding exercises for this chapter at:

http://www.ASmarterWayToLearn.com/jquery/65.html

66
SELECT THE NTH CHILD OR THE NTH CHILD OF A TYPE

Building on what you learned in the last chapter, here's how to select *any* child based on its order inside a parent element. The following code selects all images that are third children of their parents:

```
$("img:nth-child(3)")
```

Things to notice:

- The selector begins with the element type, followed by a colon— `$("img:nth-child(3)")`

- Then you write...`$("img:nth-child(3)")`

- Inside its own parentheses, you write the number: `$("img:nth-child(3)")`

The code above targets the third image in an element only if the image is the third child. This means, as you learned in the last chapter, that it doesn't necessarily target the third image. For example, if an image is the third *image* but the fifth *child* because other, non-image element types come before it in the element, it won't be selected. If you want to target the third image even though it may not be the third child, you write...

```
$("img:nth-of-type(3)")
```

Once again, these types of selectors can be used with elements of any kind—paragraphs, headings, spans, divs, etc.

Find a demo for this chapter at:
http://jsfiddle.net/ASmarterWayToLearn/78m2trwz/
Find the interactive coding exercises for this chapter at:
http://www.ASmarterWayToLearn.com/jquery/66.html

67
SELECT THE PARENTS

You've styled the default color for all the text on your page as dark grey. You display a button that lets the user change the color of the most important sections to black. When the user clicks the button, all headings, all paragraphs, and all lists inside those sections turn black. (That is, all of them turn black except for any that have been individually styled with a color.)

You define the most important sections as any divs that contain an h2 heading. Your code says, "If a div contains an h2 heading, specify black as the color for that div." This turns all the text inside that div—including headings, paragraphs, and lists—black.

```
$("button#make_black").on("click", function() {
  $("h2").parent().css("color", "black");
});
```

When the button is clicked, the code selects all parents of all h2 headings, and specifies black as the color for each of those parents. Since, in this case, the parents are divs, all text inside each of the selected divs turns black.

Find a demo for this chapter at:

http://jsfiddle.net/ASmarterWayToLearn/pvo7vcfh/

Find the interactive coding exercises for this chapter at:

http://www.ASmarterWayToLearn.com/jquery/67.html

68
SELECT THE SIBLINGS

You create an unordered list that represents different choices that the user can make. The list items are colored black. When the user clicks one of them, jQuery captures his choice. And to graphically mark all the items that *weren't* chosen, you turn all of the unchosen items grey, leaving the selected item black.

Begin by creating a class for unordered lists. Items in any list of this class get a pointer cursor so the user understands that the items are clickable:

```css
ul.choice_list li {
  color: black;
  cursor: pointer;
}
```

When the user clicks any item in a list of the "choice_list" class, this code runs:

```javascript
$("ul.choice_list li").on("click", function() {
  $(this).siblings().css("color", "#999");
});
```

When the user clicks an item, all of its siblings—that is,

all of the elements that share the same parent (**ul** in this example)—turn grey. The selected item remains black.

Find a demo for this chapter at:

http://jsfiddle.net/ASmarterWayToLearn/b04t4gng/

Find the interactive coding exercises for this chapter at:

http://www.ASmarterWayToLearn.com/jquery/68.html

69
FILTER

To select all paragraphs of the class "special," you'd write...

```
$("p.special")...
```

As an alternative, you could write...

```
$("p").filter(".special")...
```

To select the second child of all list items that have the class "sketchy," you'd write...

```
$("li.sketchy:nth-child(2))...
```

As an alternative, you could write...

```
$("li").filter(".sketchy:nth-child(2)")...
```

To select even rows in a table, you'd write...

```
$("tr:even")...
```

As an alternative, you could write...

```
$("tr").filter(":even")...
```

Find a demo for this chapter at:

http://jsfiddle.net/ASmarterWayToLearn/an3skqzc/

Find the interactive coding exercises for this chapter at:

http://www.ASmarterWayToLearn.com/jquery/69.html

70
NOT

As you know, `$("p.optional")` selects all paragraphs that have the class "optional."

To select all paragraphs that *don't* have the class "optional," you can write `$("p:not(.optional)")`...

Alternatively, you can write `$("p").not(".optional")`...

I prefer the first way of writing it, because it looks more like its positive mirror image. Again, look at the code that selects all paragraphs that have the class "optional":

```
$("p.optional")...
```

To reverse it, selecting all paragraphs that *don't* have the class optional, you add...

```
$("p:not(.optional)")...
```

- It's a colon:
  ```
  $("p:not(.optional)")...
  ```

- ...followed by not:

- ```
  $("p:not(.optional)")...
  ```

- ...and then an extra set of parentheses:

  ```
  $("p:not(.optional)")...
  ```

This is the way of doing it that I'll test you on in the exercises.

Find a demo for this chapter at:

http://jsfiddle.net/ASmarterWayToLearn/gLa3qqje/

Find the interactive coding exercises for this chapter at:

http://www.ASmarterWayToLearn.com/jquery/70.html
  ```

71

HIGHLIGHT THE ACTIVE TEXT FIELD

When the user clicks inside a text box or textarea (or Tabs into it), the field turns pale yellow. When she clicks or Tabs out, it returns to white. Here's the code that turns it yellow:

```
$("input:text, textarea").on("focus", function() {
  $(this).css("background-color", "#ffffcc");
});
```

Things to notice:

- There are two types of elements selected here, text boxes and textareas. As usual, the selectors are inside a single set of quotation marks and are separated by a comma followed by a space.

- Text boxes are selected by **$("input:text")**. Textareas are selected by a simple **$("textarea")**.

- The event is **focus**. It means when the user enters the field with a click or Tab.

The code that turns the field back to white when the user clicks or Tabs out of it is similar, with two differences:

```
$("input:text, textarea").on("blur", function() {
  $(this).css("background-color", "#fff");
});
```

- The event is **blur**, meaning that the user has clicked or Tabbed out of the field.

- The color is **#fff**—white.

Find a demo for this chapter at:

http://jsfiddle.net/ASmarterWayToLearn/6ko0nub2/

Find the interactive coding exercises for this chapter at:

http://www.ASmarterWayToLearn.com/jquery/71.html

72
EACH

Your online income tax app includes a form for claiming dependents. It has three fields: dependent spouse, dependent children, and other relatives who are dependents. You ask the user to enter a number in each field—the number of dependents he's claiming in that category. When the user clicks the "Submit" button, jQuery loops through the three fields and adds up the total dependents. This total is stored in the variable **total_dependents**. Here's the code:

```
$("form#dependents").on("submit", function() {
  var total_dependents = 0;
  $("form#dependents input:text").each(function() {
    total_dependents += parseInt($(this).val());
  });
});
```

Let me walk you through it. When the user clicks the "Submit" button...

```
$("form#dependents").on("submit", function() {
  var total_dependents = 0;
  $("form#dependents input:text").each(function() {
    total_dependents += parseInt($(this).val());
  });
});
```

...a function runs...

```
$("form#dependents").on("submit", function() {
  var total_dependents = 0;
  $("form#dependents input:text").each(function() {
    total_dependents += parseInt($(this).val());
  });
});
```

The first thing the function does is declare the variable that's going to hold the total. It starts at 0. (For more information on declaring variables, see Chapter 2 of my "A Smarter Way to Learn JavaScript.")

```
$("form#dependents").on("submit", function() {
  var total_dependents = 0;
  $("form#dependents input:text").each(function() {
    total_dependents += parseInt($(this).val());
  });
});
```

Next, all text inputs in the form are targeted:

```
$("form#dependents").on("submit", function() {
  var total_dependents = 0;
  $("form#dependents input:text").each(function() {
    total_dependents += parseInt($(this).val());
  });
});
```

Here's what's new. The code says, "Select **each** text input in turn..."

```
$("form#dependents").on("submit", function() {
  var total_dependents = 0;
  $("form#dependents input:text").each(function() {
    total_dependents += parseInt($(this).val());
  });
});
```

"...and run the same function for each one":

```
$("form#dependents").on("submit", function() {
  var total_dependents = 0;
  $("form#dependents input:text").each(function() {
    total_dependents += parseInt($(this).val());
  });
});
```

As the code loops through the three fields sequentially, the function adds the number in the current field to the running total that is being kept in the variable **total_dependents**:

```
$("form#dependents").on("submit", function() {
  var total_dependents = 0;
  $("form#dependents input:text").each(function() {
    total_dependents += parseInt($(this).val());
  });
});
```

Anything that the user enters in a form field is a text string, even if it looks like a number to you and me. All of the "numbers" in the text fields are strings, and strings can't be used in math. We need to use the JavaScript method **parseInt()**...

```
$("form#dependents").on("submit", function() {
  var total_dependents = 0;
  $("form#dependents input:text").each(function() {
    total_dependents += parseInt($(this).val());
  });
});
```

...to convert the string into an integer so it can be added to the total. For more information on the **parseInt()** method, see Chapter 28 of my "A Smarter Way to Learn JavaScript."

Find a demo for this chapter at:

http://jsfiddle.net/ASmarterWayToLearn/h2ozr433/

Find the interactive coding exercises for this chapter at:

http://www.ASmarterWayToLearn.com/jquery/72.html

73
GET INFORMATION ABOUT AN EVENT

There may be times when you know that an event has occurred but not which *type* of event has occured. Here's some code that listens for any of three types of events and reports on which type has occurred.

```javascript
$("img.clickable").on("mouseover click mouseout",
function(e) {
  var whichEvent = (e.type);
});
```

The function is triggered when the user does any of three things: mouses over the image, clicks the image, or mouses out of the image. The function identifies which of these three events has occurred and stores it in the variable **whichEvent**.

Things to notice:

- The variable **e** is in the parentheses that follow function. It refers to the event that has triggered the function. You don't *have* to name it **e**. You can use any legal variable name. But it's conventional to use **e**, which stands for "event," or use the more explicit name, **event**.

- **e.type** gives you the type of the event—the event to which the variable e refers—**mouseover**, **mouseout**, **click**, **dblclick**, **keydown**, etc.

Find a demo for this chapter at:

http://jsfiddle.net/ASmarterWayToLearn/4Lp3pfd5/

Find the interactive coding exercises for this chapter at:

http://www.ASmarterWayToLearn.com/jquery/73.html

74

SELECT ELEMENTS THAT CONTAIN A PARTICULAR STRING

Your natural-food page contains a number of products. You've asked the user to tell you what, to her, is the most important characteristic that she's looking for in natural foods. She's told you that the most important characteristic is non-GMO. Your jQuery code responds by bolding all list items on the page that contain the string "non-GMO." This is the code:

```
$("li:contains('non-GMO')").css("font-weight",
"bold");
```

Things to notice:

- The selector has the usual two layers of wrapping: parentheses enclosing quotation marks.

- It begins with the type of element, **li**.

- This is followed by a colon.

- The colon is followed by **contains**.

- The string we're looking for is in parentheses. The string is enclosed in single quotation marks.

Find a demo for this chapter at:

http://jsfiddle.net/ASmarterWayToLearn/L6pkqjvq/

Find the interactive coding exercises for this chapter at:

http://www.ASmarterWayToLearn.com/jquery/74.html

75

SELECT ELEMENTS THAT HAVE A CERTAIN ELEMENT WITHIN THEM

You have a recipe page that displays beautiful shots of the dish you're teaching the user to make. But maybe she just wants the recipe, without the pictures. Your HTML markup has placed all the images in divs, and these divs contain only images. So when she clicks the "Hide pictures" button, you select all the divs that have one or more images, and hide those divs. This is the code:

```
$("button#hide_pix").on("click", function() {
  $("div:has(img)").css("display", "none");
});
```

The form is the same as the one you learned in the last chapter, except that after the colon you write has instead of contains.

More examples:

$("p:has(a)") selects all paragraphs that have one or more links.

$("div:has(ol)") selects all divs that have one or more ordered lists.

$("h3:has(em)") selects all h3 headings that have italics.

Find a demo for this chapter at:
http://jsfiddle.net/ASmarterWayToLearn/1jkkp8ax/

Find the interactive coding exercises for this chapter at:
http://www.ASmarterWayToLearn.com/jquery/75.html

76
SELECT ELEMENTS BY ATTRIBUTE VALUE

On your webpage there are three links to Amazon. When the user clicks one of these links, you want the Amazon page to open in a new window. Normally, you'd specify this in the HMTL anchor tag: **<a href="http://www.amazon.com" target="_blank">**. But for the purposes of this example, let's say you've left it out.

```
<a href="http://www.amazon.com" target="_blank">
```

So you code this:

```
$("a[href='http://www.amazon.com']").attr("target",
"_blank");
```

The code above selects all **a** elements whose **href** attribute has a value of "http://www.amazon.com." It gives these elements a target attribute value of "_blank."

Let me go over the syntax with you:

- The attribute-value pair—
  href='http://www.amazon.com'—
  is enclosed in brackets.

- The value has to be enclosed in single
  quotation marks, since the whole selector is
  enclosed in double quotation marks.

You *could* omit the a...

```
$("a[href='http://www.amazon.com']").attr("target",
"_blank");
```

jQuery would look for *all* elements with the href value "http://www.amazon.com". This, of course, would yield only **a** elements, since no other type of element has such an attribute. So the results would be the same. But I like to spell it out, to make it more readable for humans.

More examples:

The following code targets all images with a width of 100 pixels:

```
$("img[width='100']")
```

The following code targets all inputs with a value of "single":

```
$("input[value='single']")
```

You could also use this syntax to write...

```
$("img[id='founder']")
```

...as an alternative to...

```
$("img#founder")
```

And you could write...

```
$("[class='important']")
```

...as an alternative to...

```
$(".important")
```

Find a demo for this chapter at:

http://jsfiddle.net/ASmarterWayToLearn/u8m2wnfL/

Find the interactive coding exercises for this chapter at:

http://www.ASmarterWayToLearn.com/jquery/76.html

77
SELECT ELEMENTS BY ATTRIBUTE VALUE FRAGMENT

In the last chapter, you selected all **a** elements with an **href** value of "http://www.amazon.com." But suppose your page includes links to exterior websites besides Amazon. You want all of these sites to open in a new window. You don't have to spell out the URLs for all of them, since any exterior site has a URL that begins with "http:". Just ask jQuery to select all **a** elements whose **href** attribute has a value that begins with "http:"

```
$("a[href^='http:']").attr("target", "_blank");
```

Inserting a caret before the equal sign **(^=)** says, "Select all **href** values that *begin with* "http:"

You can select fragments in other positions as well. The following code selects all images with a **src** attribute value that *ends in* ".gif."

```
$("img[src$='.gif']")...
```

The following code selects all blockquotes with a class

whose value *contains* "feature"

```
$("blockquote[class*='feature']")...
```

The code above would select, for example, all of the following blockquotes:

```
<blockquote class="featured">
<blockquote class="joke_feature">
<blockquote class="other_featured_aphorisms">
```

Find a demo for this chapter at:

http://jsfiddle.net/ASmarterWayToLearn/3ej0ew8o/

Find the interactive coding exercises for this chapter at:

http://www.ASmarterWayToLearn.com/jquery/77.html

78
DELEGATE

By now, you're an expert at listening for an event on selected elements. For example, you know, without thinking about it, how to listen for a click on all paragraphs in a particular div...

```
$("div#products p").on("click", function() {
```

But suppose you append a new paragraph to the div *after* the statement above. The new paragraph won't be included in the selection. When the user clicks it, nothing will happen. The solution is to *delegate*.

To delegate, you move the **"p"** away from the selector and make it part of the listener:

```
$("div#products").on("click", "p", function() {
```

Now all paragraphs in the div are selected, whether they're coded in the original HTML or added by jQuery.

In the above code, you know the parent of all the paragraphs you want to target. It's the div whose id is "products." But suppose you want to select, let's say, all images on the page, whether they're coded in the original HTML or added by jQuery. And you don't know all the parents of all the images. So you target the element that's the parent of them all...

```
$("body").on("click", "img", function() {
```

One more example. The following code selects all unordered list items whose class is "important" whether they're coded in the original HTML or added by jQuery:

```
$("ul").on("click", "li.important", function() {
```

Find a demo for this chapter at:

http://jsfiddle.net/ASmarterWayToLearn/nofcx26m/

Find the interactive coding exercises for this chapter at:

http://www.ASmarterWayToLearn.com/jquery/78.html

INDEX

Made in the USA
San Bernardino, CA
26 September 2017